ducks in a row
An A-Z of Offlish

ducks in a row
An A-Z of Offlish

The definitive guide to Office English

Carl Newbrook

First published in 2005 by
Short Books
15 Highbury Terrace
London N5 1UP

10 9 8 7 6 5 4 3 2 1

A CIP catalogue record for this book
is available from the British Library.

ISBN 1-904977-35-9

Printed and bound in Great Britain by William Clowes Ltd, Beccles, Suffolk

To Mary Newbrook and Irene Newbrook

'But he doesn't have anything on!' the entire crowd cried at last. The Emperor cringed, because he thought they were right, but then he reasoned, 'I have to make it through the procession.' He held himself even prouder than before, and the chamberlains walked along carrying the train that was not there at all.

Hans Christian Andersen, *The Emperor's New Clothes*

One of the most salient features of our culture is that there is so much bullshit. Everyone knows this.

Harry G. Frankfurt, *On Bullshit*

Introduction

The Rise of Office English or Offlish

We live in an administrated world. If we don't actually work in an office of some kind, our lives, almost certainly, will be organised and governed by people who do. Just as we have all mutated into consumers, so we are now all managed.

The office is the common backdrop, and yet it is an environment that is not much written about. Where, for example, is the great novel of life in the office? Ricky Gervais and Stephen Merchant's *The Office* gained a huge following because it was hilarious and beautifully crafted, but also because, to those who do work in an office, it was horribly recognisable. It showed that the essential nature of relationships in the office is based on a level of deference that would shame a medieval court; that boredom, evasiveness, manipulation and politicking are endemic; and that truth-telling is not encouraged. This is a picture that is not generally reflected in management handbooks or the optimistic writings of business gurus.

Something that was not developed in the series, however, was that the office has spawned its own extraordinarily diverse comic language: Office English or Offlish. This is an unappetising stew of acronyms, adages, catchphrases, clichés, euphemisms, jargon, ugly neologisms, bogus phrases and slang that is now prevalent in offices everywhere. It is language that is not designed for clear communication. It is the language of avoidance, of hoodwinking, of half-truths and outright lies. It is the language of bullshit. Much of it is risible and, while we all recognise it when it is pointed out, it is, nonetheless, insidious. And there is more of it now than ever before. It is ubiquitous. Indeed, in recent years it has also begun to colonise other areas, notably the press and television, so that it is scarcely an exaggeration to claim Offlish as our common public language. Turn on the radio, open a newspaper, switch on the television, and examples of Offlish nonsense are abundant.

Ducks in a Row is a lighthearted lexicon that provides navigation through this new language of Offlish, and an understanding of how it is used. It is, essentially, a list of words and phrases that should be avoided, or at best used sparingly, in speech and writing. It is not a grammatical primer (much as I respect the grammarian's forensic intelligence), a general jeremiad (as English is ceaselessly evolving) or a grumpy lecture (well, perhaps, just a little bit). Each word or phrase has a rating to show its offensiveness – a subjective and unscientific score out of five – and a section giving examples of usage as well as typical users, such as the Ambitious manager, the Machiavellian manager and the Unironic manager; the CEO, management consultant or Sales manager. In addition, it is cross-referenced so that it can be read by theme.

My intention is to amuse and entertain, but *Ducks in a Row* is also a guide to identify those who are enthusiastic or persistent users of Offlish. They are the linguistic equivalent of Typhoid Mary; and as Offlish is highly contagious, it is vital that these people, whoever they are and wherever they are, are mocked, ridiculed and undermined in order to prevent its spread. I hope, therefore, that *Ducks in a Row* will function as a kind of humorous inoculation. I speak with experience as someone who was once asked, literally, to sing from the same corporate hymn sheet. But, as the Unironic manager would say, 'At this moment in time,[§] that's another story . . . '

§ 'Time, at this moment in' is, and I hope that this is uncontentious, a five-star phrase.

A-Z
= phrase: the alphabet

From the beginning to the end; the whole story.

Usage **** – *Unironic managers* underlining their intention to examine every aspect of a problem: 'We need to look at everything from beginning to end, the whole shooting match, and get our *ducks in a row*. This is an *A–Z* scenario, *guys*.'

See also **Ducks in a row**; **Guys**; **Unironic manager**; **Z**

Absolutely!
= interj: completely; unconditionally

A word that demands an exclamation mark!

Usage ***** – Everyone, everywhere, constantly. This is the correct Offlish term§ to express enthusiastic agreement (or at least to pretend to express enthusiastic agreement). *Unironic managers* will often add the superfluous rider: 'I hear what you are saying!'

See also **Enthusiasm**; **Unironic manager**

§ 'Definitely!', 'Exactly!' and 'Precisely!' are common variations.

Accelerator, take one's foot off the
= phrase: to reduce speed

A foolish error that results in progress that is slower than anticipated.

Usage*** - The phrase sounds forceful, but its vagueness makes it a useful means of declaring general responsibility without accepting personal culpability. It is, therefore, ideal for delivering all kinds of '*bad news*': the Chairman briefing the City or shareholders on a set of poor results; senior managers reporting to the board; junior managers grovelling to their boss. (A popular variation is 'taking one's eye off the ball'.)

See also **News, bad**

Act
= n: a performance

Often hard to follow.

Usage*** - *Unironic managers*; downtrodden but watchfully respectful managers.

See also **Monster**; **Unironic manager**

Act together, get our
= phrase: display organisation and purposefulness

A common threat or plea.

Usage** - *Sales managers* as one of their principal means of encouragement to their subordinates; also desperate managers lacking in confidence begging for assistance from their *teams*.

See also **Sales manager**; **Team**

Action
= v: to act; implement; make happen

In the office the saying 'Actions speak louder than words' is widely respected.

Usage***** - The transmogrification of '*action*' from a noun into a verb is now so widespread in Offlish usage as to be unchallengeable, the standard English equivalents – 'do' or 'complete' – being regarded as too weedy for the muscular needs of the office. The enthusiastic wielding of this unlovely term will, however, mark out colleagues who might best be avoided, even if this can only be on social occasions. It is used in *meetings* by managers and executives everywhere to underline their vigorous determination. It is also a favourite of jargon-spewing *management consultants* as well as *Ambitious managers* (faking interest as usual) and *Unironic managers*, who are all Offlish devotees: 'Who is going to *action* this?'/ 'Can we look at the *actioning* of this PDQ?' There is also an ugly adjective: 'What's *actionable* from the *agenda*?' '*Drive*', '*land*', '*nail*' and '*own*', which are all equally unattractive, are often used as substitutes.

See also **Agenda**; **Ambitious manager**; **Drive**; **Land**; **Management consultant**; **Meeting**; **Nail**; **Own**; **Unironic manager**

Action-oriented

= adj: predisposed to action

A mongrel term: the offspring of fashion and baloney.

Usage ***** – Unblushing executives who don't care if they are talking nonsense; pretentious, jargon-ridden job adverts written by empty-headed *HR managers*; eager-to-please candidates who hope that Offlish will make them appear in-the-club, business-like, pliant and, therefore, suitable for corporate employment; on-the-make managers who use Offlish gobbledegook to show their seeming *commitment* to the cause; lazy managers who take refuge in Offlish rather than thinking for themselves; also *Unironic managers* who don't know any better. (A similar term is 'target-oriented'.)

See also **Commitment**; **Human Resources manager**; **Unironic manager**

Acumen

= n: insight

A fallible idol.

Usage ** – In job adverts for a large number of roles and positions, where it is a synonym for 'intelligence' or 'competence'. It is also favoured by journalists to describe successful executives; however, once the executive is perceived to be failing, the same quality becomes recklessness or ignorance.

See also **Hero-to-zero**

Age, come of

= phrase: to reach maturity

A rite-of-passage that should be celebrated with great ceremony.

Usage * – Managers, especially *No-nonsense managers*, who are unable to resist football terminology, metaphors and analogies (a body of language otherwise known as *Premiership English*): 'He did the business, all right. He *came of age* with that project, he did.'

See also **No-nonsense manager**; **Premiership English**

Agenda

= n: listing of business for a meeting to discuss

A charade played to elaborate, difficult-to-follow rules that, in addition, vary from one locality to another.

Usage * – Managers everywhere.

See also **Agenda, hidden**

Agenda, hidden

= n: a secret plan

Quantum physics, for those with sufficient knowledge and

intelligence to understand its principles, has posited the existence of parallel universes; so it is in the office also.

Usage **** – Outraged managers who have been outwitted by a *Machiavellian* colleague; exhausted managers who have given up the fight.

See also **Machiavellian manager**

Ah!
= interj: an expression of surprise

The sound of revelation.

Usage *** – Guilty managers who have been rumbled:
– 'Isn't this the same information you presented last week? And wasn't it wrong then, too?'
– '*Ah!*'

See also **Oh!**

Airhead
= n: an unintelligent person; a scatterbrain

In the office there is a place for everyone.

Usage ** – Managers mocking a *colleague* (or '*space cadet*') whose powers of disorganisation are a constant source of amusement and encouragement: 'What an *airhead*! He's on another planet, that one.'

See also **Colleague**; **Muppet**; **Space cadet**

Alarm bells ringing, set
= phrase: a warning

A loud and painful sound that, nonetheless, is often ignored.

Usage ** – A favourite expression of *Alan Hansen* when describing a defence that has had a 'lucky escape' – and therefore a favourite phrase of the *No-nonsense manager* in response to any untoward event. It should also be audible on any occasion when anyone suggests that the job, project or task in hand offers *opportunities* for *personal growth*. Hand-wringing *Training managers* and unscrupulous *HR managers* are especially prone to such lapses of taste and decorum.

See also **Growth, personal**; **Alan Hansen**; **No-nonsense manager**; **Opportunity**; **Training manager**

Aligned
= adj: placed in a row; showing unity or togetherness

The company line.

Usage** – It is a favourite word of the chummy, we're-all-in-this-together *CEO* in order to demonstrate to the entire company that teamwork is vital to success at all levels of the organisation: 'You couldn't get a cigarette paper between the *guys* on the board. We are *aligned*.'

See also **CEO**; **Ducks in a row**; **Guys**

A list, the
= n: the most important people

As anyone will tell you: 'If you have to ask . . .'

Usage** – Chairmen talking up the company; *players* matter-of-factly; *PR managers* wishfully; also envious managers who cannot understand that their abundant and obvious talents have not been universally recognised by rapid leapfrogging promotions and substantial salary increases.

See also **Player**; **Public Relations manager**

All-singing-all-dancing
= adj: complete; impressive

A promise of entertainment that is rarely fulfilled.

Usage** – A term (via vaudeville or the musical hall) used especially by *Marketing managers* to signal that every effort has been made to include all the relevant data in a particular report, presentation or piece of work. It is also used regularly by *IT managers* to describe high-quality products (or those claimed to be 'state of the art') such as computer software that has new and up-to-date features ('*all the bells and whistles*').

See also **Full monty**; **Kitchen sink**; **IT manager**; **Marketing manager**; **Whistles, bells and**

Always-on
= adj: continually alert

A stance that announces itself in an unmistakable manner.

Usage***** – This is a dark term that should trigger a Pavlovian response: an immediate and unrenounceable distrust of the user. Anyone prepared to use the phrase without an ironic inflection is almost certain to be a thousand-yard-stare *workaholic* sociopath whose entire existence begins and ends with the office. Such individuals are dangerous and should, if at all possible, be avoided. They can only bring trouble; or worse, generate even more work for you. It is used most frequently by the *Hungry manager* who never turns off his BlackBerry – 'I'm an *always-on* kind of a person' – and in job adverts for sales positions: 'You will be expected to have an *always-on* attitude.'

See also **CrackBerry**; **Full-on**; **Hungry manager**; **24/7**; **Workaholic**

Ambassador
= n: a diplomatic officer of the highest standing; an official representative

A ceremonial position that demands the highest standards of probity, tact and discretion. As the old joke has it: an honest man sent abroad to lie for his country.

Usage** – Candidates at interviews grotesquely exaggerating their previous experience; job adverts for senior positions – 'Diplomatic, persuasive, consultative, articulate, energetic, mature, flexible, a strong leadership style and an *ambassador* for the business' (translation: 'And if you can change water into wine, that would be great') – and not-so-senior positions where it generally has the meaning: 'Someone who talks to customers/clients and therefore must be able to mind their corporate *Ps and Qs.*'

See also **Ps and Qs**

Ambition
= n: aspiration for success; an aim or goal

A much-maligned quality that is exemplified by the rich and successful.

Usage** – Executives describing a new project; in job adverts for senior positions: 'You will be a doer who consistently demonstrates *ambition*, *drive* and determination.' It is also used as an all-purpose slur by embittered managers who have been passed over repeatedly for promotion. Moreover, it is a characteristic ascribed to female *colleagues* far more often than male *colleagues*.

See also **Colleague**; **Drive**

Anorak
= n: a boring person who is an obsessive *enthusiast* (from the Inuktitut for a hooded jacket)

An individual with specialist knowledge.

Usage** – Managers everywhere of their IT *colleagues* who are widely seen as problem-makers as well as problem-solvers.

See also **Colleague**; **Enthusiasm**; **Geek**; **Nerd**

Ambitious manager

The record of the *Ambitious manager* (or 'Bullshitter' as he is colloquially known) is usually unblemished, as he has a knack for being in the right place at the right time. He is a counterfeiter and scene-stealer, his goal is corporate advancement and he will let no one get in his way. He has an uncanny, chameleon-like ability to mimic the tone, views and vocabulary of the most senior person in the room. Although his *sense of humour* is, at best, weak, he is likely to have a loud and braying laugh to better appreciate the quips and sallies of those higher up the corporate *ladder*. He has no opinions of his own; thus for him Offlish offers a resource and a lexicon to ease his passage through the working day and to further his career. Although, on occasions, his chutzpah must be applauded, he is unscrupulous, devious and wholly untrustworthy. He is loathed by all and should, if at all possible, be avoided.[§]

See also **Action**; **Ante**; **Bed, put to**; **Brand**; **Catch-22**; **Change, step**; **Consumer agenda**; **Cost-effective**; **Drains-up, pull up the manhole cover and have a**; **Drive**; **80/20 rule**; **Enthusiasm**; **Fences, mend**; **Flip side**; **Hobson's Choice**; **Holistic**; **Humour, sense of**; **KPIs**; **Ladder**; **Out, up or**; **Picture, big**; **Proactive**; **Problem**; **Rocket science**; **Shop, talking**; **Stack up**; **Sword, double-edged**; **Team, catalyst**; **Whistles, bells and**

[§] The collective noun for *Ambitious managers* is a display.

Answer, straight
= n: a candid response

Could I get back to you on that?

Usage*** – Despairing managers: 'You just can't get a *straight answer* from anyone in this place.'

See also **Feedback**; **Honest, to be**; **Input**; **No**; **Yes**

Ante
= n: a stake

Invariably increased.

Usage*** – A gambling term with a precise meaning that is used imprecisely in the office. It is, therefore, simultaneously as useful to the *Ambitious manager* who can appear '*up for it*' as to the manager who has lost his way but knows that 'rattling a few cages' will at least give the appearance of control to his *team* and, even more importantly, of *commitment* to his boss: 'No pussyfooting. We're upping the *ante* on this one and going for broke.'

See also **Ambitious manager**; **Commitment**; **Hungry manager**; **Team**; **Tits out**; **Up for it?**

Apples with apples
= phrase: comparing like with like

The only valid starting point for any kind of financial analysis. After all, it has served greengrocers well for generations.

Usage** – *Finance managers* dismissing the arguments of non–finance managers: 'Hold on. You're not comparing *apples with apples*. This is an apples and oranges situation'; also under-fire *CEOs* dismissing the reasoned arguments of well-prepared financial journalists.

See also **CEO**; **Finance manager**

Appropriate
= adj: suitable

Mostly used inappropriately.

Usage * – Now in widespread usage everywhere. In the office it has come to be a mealy-mouthed catch-all substitute for coherent argument. 'Is this an *appropriate* use of time/money/resources?' may sound like a good question, but will often conceal a dazzling vacuity of intelligence and knowledge. It is especially popular with PC-fixated *HR managers* as well as *Unironic managers* for whom the lexicon of Offlish is their entire language and an effective replacement for thinking.

See also **Human Resources manager**; **Unironic manager**

Armageddon
= n: a battle on a large scale (in the New Testament, Revelations 16:16, it is the final battle between good and evil)

A setback.

Usage **** – *Dramatic managers* for whom *everything* is on the grandest scale; hysterical *PR managers* who habitually raid the lexicon of *hype*.

See also **Doomsday scenario**; **Dramatic manager**; **Hype**; **Public Relations manager**

Articulate inadequate
= n: a person who speaks well but is not competent

Today oratory is a largely obsolete art suitable only for high ceremonial occasions.§

Usage ** – Managers damning a (more eloquent) *colleague*: 'He's nothing but an *articulate inadequate*. A hot air merchant. He can talk the talk all right. But can he *walk the walk*?'

See also **Colleague**; **Walk the walk**

§ Such as the more formal leaving do.

ASAP

= acronym: As Soon As Possible

A very small unit of time.[§]

Usage**** – For some impatient managers an insufficiency:
'I need this *ASAP*. Like yesterday.'

[§] A fit subject for the letters page of the *Guardian*: 'The time taken by the driver behind to notice the light is green'; 'The time between a pear being ripe and spoiled', and so on and so on.

Ask, big

= n: a difficult task

Every day in the office there is a mountain to climb.

Usage*** – A phrase via *Premiership English* popular with *No-nonsense managers* who are unable to resist football terminology: 'We'll have to up the work-rate and get amongst them. But it's a *big ask*. There's no question about that.'[§]

See also **No-nonsense manager**; **Premiership English**

[§] This last phrase - 'There's no question about that' – is a favourite of the commentator John Motson.

Aspirational

= adj: a desire to achieve

A word that aspires to meaning but often falls short.

Usage*** – Its optimistic connotations make it a favourite with all managers, but especially *Brand* and *Marketing managers* who like to sprinkle it into their patter and presentations like a kind of Disneyfied magic dust: 'Think new. Think aspirational.'
It is also at the foggy centre of the philosophy of the *Californian manager*.

See also **Brand manager**; **Californian manager**; **Marketing manager**

Assertive
= adj: confident; direct

A highly valued modern trait that is a cause of great misery.

Usage* – Biting *Sales managers* for whom this style is a badge of honour; in job adverts for sales positions: 'You will be forthright and *assertive*' (translation: 'Are you a thuggish, foot-in-the-door, always-have-the-last-word, motormouth?'); also *Training managers* organising courses in 'skills gaps'.

See also **Sales manager**; **Training manager**

Asset
= n: an item of property; a valuable or useful thing

A tradeable item and one that, in changed circumstances, can become redundant or useless.

Usage*** – A word used most frequently by *CEOs* in interviews with the press, at company conferences and in corporate literature: 'Our *people* are our greatest *asset* ...'; as well as by cynical *HR* directors and *managers*: '... but it's a fact of life that in order to achieve maximum competitiveness hard facts must be faced and hard decisions taken.'

See also **Downsize**; **Human Resources manager**; **People**; **Restructure**; **Talent, pool of**

At the end of the day
= phrase: in conclusion

... it's only money.

Usage**** – *Unironic managers* as the preface to another stating-the-bleedin'-obvious summary; moralising senior managers who see themselves as model dispensers of folksy down-home wisdom: 'Well, it's all about *the numbers at the end of the day*.'

See also **Bean counter**; **Numbers, the**; **Unironic manager**

Ron Atkinson

The creator of Ronglish. Beefy defender, flamboyant manager, perma-tanned former pundit and the originator of a host of *Premiership English* neologisms that have become the backbone of the vocabulary of the *No-nonsense manager* for whom, despite his fall from grace, he is a *mentor* and *inspiration*.

See also **Comics, reading too many; Football, fantasy; Inspirational; Mentor; No-nonsense manager; Pear-shaped, go; Premiership English; Stall, set out one's**

Attitude, can-do
= phrase: positive, enthusiastic stance

For some a term of the highest approbation.

Usage ***** – *Sales managers* who see life in the office as a perpetual striving and know exactly the characteristics they want from their '*troops*'. It is salutary, however, to remember that all the infamous tyrants and dictators of history could also be described as possessing a similar disposition.

See also **Sales manager; Troops, the; Versatile**

Autonomy
= n: self-government

A state of independence enjoyed by mavericks.

Usage *** – Cynical *HR managers*; wide-eyed *Californian managers*; in job adverts for all kind of positions: 'You will have a high level of *autonomy* as well as the resources to deliver from *strategy* through to implementation' (translation: 'But when your boss says "JUMP!", the correct answer is: "How high, Sir?"').

See also **Californian manager**; **Human Resources manager**;
Maverick; **Strategy**

Axe
= n & v: a tool for cutting or chopping; to terminate

An implement that requires regular and careful attention in
order to retain its sharpness.

Usage *** - Fearful managers and *HR managers*, privately.

See also **Card, red**; **Go, let**; **Human Resources manager**;
Wood, dead

Backstabber
= n: a devious and underhand person

A brave individual who is prepared to take action to defend
himself and acts according to principle at all times.

Usage ** - Severely injured managers who have discovered that
they allied themselves with the wrong individual or clan at the
wrong time. Many offices resemble warring mafia families or an
Italian Renaissance city state (but without the art).

See also **Machiavellian manager**

Bag of snakes, mad as a
= phrase: eccentric or unconventional

A mesmerising sight.

Usage * - Managers - originality being, more often than not,
misunderstood - describing a (more successful) *colleague*.
In the hurly-burly of the office it is useful to have a supply of
'mad as . . .' analogies.

See also **Box of frogs, mad as a**; **Fish, mad as a jumping**;
Python, mad as a writhing; **Swing bin, mad as a**

Bake

= v: to cook using a dry heat

A domestic skill much admired in the office.

Usage*** – Managers, especially *Finance managers*, demanding that an improvement is not squandered: 'We need to *bake* this into *the numbers* otherwise we're in danger of having to *reinvent the wheel*.' The standard English equivalent is 'fix [in place]'.

See also **Finance manager**; **Numbers, the**; **Wheel, reinvent the**

Ball, curve

= n: an unexpected event

Thrown at dizzying speed.

Usage*** – Bruised and humiliated managers who didn't see it coming (but think that an Americanism – via the language of baseball – makes them sound *cool*).§

See also **Cool!**; **Plate, step up to the**

§ Offlish users who grew up watching *Friends* and *Sex in the City* will often use words and phrases such as 'dude', 'dumb ass', 'go figure', 'like whatever', 'outta here', 'sooooo last week/month/year', 'yadda, yadda, yadda' and 'yeah, right'.

Ball, drop the

= phrase: make a mistake

A common problem in the office as well as, historically, for Scottish goalkeepers.

Usage** – Managers complaining that they have been let down: 'Everything was hunky-dory until the board/Finance/IT/ Marketing/Operations/Publicity/Sales *dropped the ball*.'

See also **Baton, pass the**

Ballbreaker

= n: a disciplinarian

A female manager with a firm hand.

Usage ** – Male managers everywhere on their female peers, but especially *No-nonsense managers* who are still struggling with the political and social changes for women that took place in the 19th and 20th centuries.

See also **Bombshell**; **No-nonsense manager**

Ballpark

= adj & n: an estimation; a stadium

A huge area set aside for playing all kinds of office games.

Usage ** – Time-pressed ill-prepared managers; *Lackadaisical managers*; *No-nonsense managers* who do not have the patience or intelligence to bother with a financial analysis; also *Finance managers* committing professional hara-kiri: 'It's still a bit of a *ballpark figure* at the moment. It's somewhere between 50 quid and a round million . . . Er, we haven't finished *crunching the numbers* yet.'

See also **Finance manager**; **Guesstimate**; **Lackadaisical manager**; **No-nonsense manager**; **Number crunching**

Balls

= n: courage

Often claimed to be a necessary attribute for all successful individuals – both male and female.

Usage*** – Hard-pressed *CEOs* encouraging the board; senior managers encouraging middle managers; middle managers encouraging junior managers; *No-nonsense managers* and *Sales managers* at all times.

See also **CEO**; **Cojones**; **No-nonsense manager**; **Sales manager**

Balls in the air

= phrase: a juggling act

An entertainment suitable for children.

Usage *** – Harassed managers who have dropped something; self-satisfied managers who have not. Certain circus skills are a prerequisite for success in the office.

See also **Hat; Multitask**

Balls-up

= n: a muddle caused by incompetence

The inevitable result of the intervention of a *colleague*.

Usage *** – Managers everywhere.

See also **Colleague; Shambles**

Banana skin

= n: the outer part of a banana

A comic book hazard and a common threat to stability in the office.

Usage ** – Journalists seeing the potential for misfortune (and hoping for a story); executives acknowledging the potential for misfortune (and hoping that it can be avoided); managers seeing the potential for a hilarious head-over-heels crash from a *colleague*.

See also **Colleague**

Bandwidth

= n: the capacity of a communication channel

Always too small to be fully effective.

Usage *** – A vogue word from the baffling world of IT used by executives and senior managers adding an unnecessary technical gloss to a simple statement: 'We need more *bandwidth* to achieve top-line growth.'

See also **IT manager**

Barrel, over a

= phrase: an exposed situation

An uncomfortable position that often results in the granting of concessions.

Usage ** – Gleeful managers looking on; stoical managers who hope that the punishment, though painful, will at least be delivered speedily.

See also **Catch-22**

Basics, back to

= phrase: the most important; the essential

A panacea.

Usage **** – A phrase popularised by the beleaguered Conservative Prime Minister John Major that is befogged and almost meaningless. It is used regularly, therefore, by executives, directors and other managers in difficult circumstances who have run out of ideas but who wish to appear statesmanlike and purposeful.

See also **Bread and butter**; **Core**; **Knitting, stick to the**; **No-nonsense manager**; **Principles, first**; **Sales manager**

Baton, pass the

= phrase: to hand over

A skill requiring a great deal of practice to perfect.

Usage ** – Managers reflecting on how their hard work has been sabotaged by an incompetent *colleague*: 'I *passed the baton*. All the eejit had to do was run with it ...'

See also **Ball, drop the**; **Colleague**

Bean counter
= n: an accountant

A master of an arcane art.

Usage *** – Managers speaking of a workmate in the Finance department for whom numbers express all the order, clarity and harmony that is absent from normal life. An influential individual often blamed for all manner of corporate ills (business *guru Tom Peters*, for example, has talked about the 'tyranny of the *bean counters*'); he is, however, an unlikely candidate for self-reflection or vivacious conversation: '*At the end of the day*, when all's said and done, it's all about *the numbers ...*'

See also **At the end of the day**; **Finance manager**; **Guru**; **Numbers, the**; **Number crunching**; **Tom Peters**

Beans, spill the
= phrase: to reveal the facts

Unless there are large amounts of money involved, an inadvisable course of action.

Usage ** – Managers demanding that a subordinate passes on useful information.

Bed, get into
= phrase: to form a partnership; liaise

A metaphor; or, at least for the most part, a metaphor.

Usage **** – Executives everywhere; *No-nonsense managers* with a smirk.

See also **No-nonsense manager**

Bed in
= v: to integrate

A process by which time is shown to be a great healer.

Usage *** – Managers everywhere, but especially *IT managers* who wish that a question had not been asked, who don't have the detail to give a complete answer or are badly in need of time to find *any* kind of answer. It is useful jargon, as it can cover myriad circumstances and does not commit the user to anything other than a show of laudable optimism: 'No, it's not a disaster. Yes, there are teething problems. It just needs a bit of time to *bed in*' (translation: 'It's a disaster').

See also **Hiccup**; **IT manager**; **Strategy**

Bed, put to
= phrase: to complete a task

Often proves to be more difficult than dealing with a demented toddler.

Usage *** – Managers everywhere, in many different contexts, to indicate that an activity or piece of work has been, or needs to be, completed; *Ambitious managers* faking interest; *Unironic managers* routinely: 'Let's get this one *put to bed, ASAP*.'

See also **Ambitious manager**; **ASAP**; **Tick in the box**; **Unironic manager**

Behind, get
= v: to demonstrate commitment or enthusiasm

A blandishment or workaday threat.

Usage *** – Managers and executives everywhere; notably *Sales managers*: '*Guys*, we need to *get behind* this one and pull out all *the stops*.'

See also **Guys**; **Sales manager**; **Stops, the**

Bête noire

= n: a person or thing particularly disliked

A beast suitable for a menagerie.

Usage* – *Thesaurus managers* (with a flourish on the Gallic 'r').

See also **Thesaurus manager**

Bigwig

= n: an influential person

A *player.*

Usage* – Directors with a wary respect for a business opponent; deferential managers.

See also **Cheese, big**; **Fromage, grand**; **Player**; **Shaker, mover and**

Black arts

= n: magic invoking the Devil's aid and used for evil purposes

Expertise, often involving an apprenticeship, that can come at a considerable cost.

Usage* – Journalists describing corporate machinations around takeover bids and boardroom reshuffles; *PR managers* privately; out-flanked executives criticising a rival's underhand tactics; managers who have been comprehensively outmanoeuvred by a *Machiavellian* colleague.

See also **Machiavellian manager**; **Public Relations manager**

Blamestorm

= n: a round of accusations

The outcome of any review.

Usage**** – Exhausted or exhilarated managers – depending on the outcome – reporting examples of internecine strife:

'It wasn't a *meeting*. It was a *blamestorm*.There was literally *blood on the floor*.'

See also **Floor, blood on the**; **Meeting**

Blank canvas
= n: an empty space

A valueless item or a work of art.

Usage **** – Beware: the proffered '*blank canvas*' is never pristine.The phrase is used regularly by executives and senior managers who need a subordinate to solve a *problem* they don't have the answer to (and to take responsibility for the *problem*). A 'blank cheque' should be treated with the same suspicion.

See also **Problem**; **Thinking, blue-sky**

Blue chip
= n: the most reliable shares

Share prices may go down as well as up. Always speak to an independent adviser.

Usage ** – The volatility of the market has exposed the fatuity of the very notion of *blue chip* untouchability, yet the phrase is still used regularly as a kind of talisman in the hope that some of the magic might rub off on the user. It is regularly trotted out by executives in press interviews and in briefings to the City, where the phrase signals the company's never-ending search for the highest possible standards.

Boat, in the same
= phrase: in a similar situation

A situation ill-suited to sufferers of claustrophobia.

Usage *** – Beleaguered *CEOs* threatening the board: 'If *I* go down, then *you* all go down with me. Don't forget, we're *in the* *same boat*'; scheming *Machiavellian managers*; wheedling workmates; also *Training managers* encouraging everyone to 'pull together in the same direction'.

See also **CEO**; **Machiavellian manager**; **Training manager**

Boat, rock the
= phrase: overturn the status quo

A very dangerous activity in choppy waters and, therefore, only undertaken by the reckless or foolhardy.

Usage**** – Executives and senior managers issuing a warning; the *Worldly-wise manager* offering advice.

See also **Worldly-wise manager**

Bomb
= n: an explosive device

Invariably ticking.

Usage** – Concerned managers who know too much, or think they know too much; uninvolved managers excitedly looking forward to the coming conflagration.

Bombshell
= n: unexpected news; a bomb

Once in a while a ticking *bomb does* explode ...

Usage** – An overused term employed by *Dramatic managers* to describe any kind of *change* in the office: for example, a sudden fall in the value of the company's shares; a new pension scheme; the announcement of a phased introduction of a new re-ordering process for stationery; the absence of almond croissants in the canteen, and so on and so on ... §

See also **Armageddon**; **Bomb**; **Change**; **Dramatic manager**; **No-nonsense manager**

§ *No-nonsense managers* will always describe a woman with blonde hair (or even highlights) as a '*blonde bombshell*'.

Bottom line, the
= n: the final profit; most important; the essential

The profit accruing once all the costs have been calculated: the purpose of any company.

Usage ***** – A favourite expression of self-important executives and senior managers who will use it to justify any kind of unpalatable *change*. It is also used in *meetings* by all kinds of manager as a means of bringing an uncomfortable debate to a close. It is, in fact, a useful phrase to justify just about anything.

See also **Bread and butter**; **Change**; **Stack up**

Bouncebackability
= n: resilience

An essential quality for the successful man or woman.

Usage * – A *Premiership English* term (recently coined by the Crystal Palace manager Iain Dowie) and picked up adroitly by the *No-nonsense manager*: 'When the chips are down and the heat is on, you need to show a bit of *bouncebackability*.'

See also **No-nonsense manager**; **Premiership English**

Box of frogs, mad as a
= phrase: eccentric or unconventional

An entertaining sight.

Usage** – Managers – originality being, more often than not, misunderstood – describing a (more successful) colleague. In the hurly-burly of the office it is useful to have a supply of 'mad as . . .' analogies.

See also **Bag of snakes, mad as a**; **Colleague**; **Fish, mad as a**;
Python, mad as a writhing; **Swing bin, mad as a**

Box, thinking outside the
= phrase: an unconventional approach

Usage ***** – Central to the self-image of the *Brand* and
Marketing manager, but also used often by anyone who likes
to present themselves as unconventional and *inspirational*.
It is also regularly seen in job adverts for creative roles and
demanded by managers in response to all kinds of *problems*, yet
is rarely acted on: 'We need to go beyond the conventional
wisdom and *think outside the box*.' If you choose your moment
well, you may provoke a smile by suggesting that real '*thinking
outside the box*' would involve working *9–5* with an hour for
lunch, longer holidays, better facilities such as a café, gym and
creche as well as clear job roles, regular salary reviews and
profit-sharing. Alternatively, if you choose your moment badly,
this could provoke violent hostility or even a *P45*.

See also **Brand manager**; **CEO**; **Greenfield opportunity**;
Inspirational; **Marketing manager**; **9–5**; **P45**; **Percentages,
play the**; **Problem**; **Square, thinking outside the**; **Thinking,
blue-sky**; **Thinking, lateral**; **Unthinkable, thinking the**

Boys, big
= n: influential people

Properly feared in the playground and possessed thereafter of
a natural hauteur.

Usage *** – Cowed managers; aggressive managers for whom the
office is a Darwinian battleground where, in the race to be the
fittest, it is the '*big boys*' who tend to win: 'If you want to join

the *big boys,* then you've got to act the part.'

Boys, jobs for the
= phrase: promotion through favouritism

A principle, now widely seen as outdated, that nonetheless has been effective for many family firms and political dynasties.

Usage** – Embittered managers (especially women and men with regional accents) who have been passed over for promotion.

See also **PLU**

Brainstorm
= n & v: a meeting to generate new ideas; to generate new ideas

A horrible sight and a destructive event.

Usage*** – Senior managers who believe in '*making it happen*'; senior managers who can't '*make it happen*'.

See also **Happen, make it**; **Headbang**

Brand
= n: corporate identity; a distinguishing mark; a torch

A light held aloft and carefully tended to guide us through this vale of tears.

Usage***** – There now exists a vast number of books on the nature of *brands* and branding, and whole organisations exist to help other organisations manage their *brand* more effectively. One common definition has it that a *brand* is the sum of the feelings and ideas that are held by the customers of that organisation towards the organisation. *Brand managers,* however, talk in an impenetrable patois of their own creation, are prone to statements of a gnomic nature – 'The *brand* is us and we are the *brand*' – and are not comfortable with facts, figures and quotidian realities. *Ambitious managers* will invariably learn one or two of the words or phrases most frequently used by the company's executives to describe the *brand* (or 'proposition' or 'message' or 'story' or '*vision*') so that they can drop them into conversations in order to impress a superior. Everyone else uses the word either mockingly or with embarrassment.

See also **Ambitious manager**; **Brand manager**; **Tom Peters**; **On-brand**; **Throw the baby out with the bath water, don't**; **Vision**

Brand manager

His self-confidence is total, his commitment to the *brand* unchallengeable and his detachment from the world complete (he is known colloquially to his colleagues as a 'brandroid'). He is responsible for the massively expensive corporate rebranding exercises – via a 'brandstorming' process – such as the calamitous morphing of the Royal Mail into Consignia. He is also the creator of 'positioning' statements that aim to embody the company's 'values' and that will be used on all corporate literature and parroted by the board and senior managers at every opportunity – such as Enron's 'Learn the power of why'. These statements he will describe grandly as the Customer Offer Vision or the Take Home Message. Typically, his thought is convoluted and his vocabulary gibberish, and therefore normal conversation with him is impossible. He is reviled by everyone and he should, if at all possible, be avoided.[§]

See also **Aspirational**; **Box, thinking outside the**; **Brand**; **Custodian**; **Headbang**; **Off-brand**; **On-brand**; **Square, thinking outside the**; **Thinking, lateral**; **Tipping point**; **USP**; **Vision**

[§] The collective noun for *Brand managers* is an abracadabra or abstraction.

Bread and butter

= n: the mainstay; reliable

Often presented as a tastier and more nutritious diet than that offered by the finest restaurateur.

Usage *** – *No-nonsense managers* seeking to demonstrate in a typically vigorous brawn-over-brain fashion their understanding (almost always misconceived) of the essence of the business.

See also **Basics, back to**; **Bottom line, the**; **Core**; **Non-core**; **No-nonsense manager**; **Rocket science**

Breed, best in

= phrase: finest in a category

A pat on the head is the appropriate reward.

Usage *** – A verbal curlicue ('best in class' is a variation) for executives and senior managers, who without this handy phrase would perhaps find it necessary to announce that a new product was 'probably a little bit better than the last one of its type (although it may need a bit of time to get established)'.

See also **World-class**; **Hype**

Bridges, build

= phrase: make connections or allies

A tedious, ongoing, never-ending task in the office.

Usage ** – Managers everywhere, regularly and reluctantly; *Californian managers* for whom conflict is anathema: 'We need to create rapport, avoid silos and *build bridges*.'

See also **Californian manager**

Bright-eyed and bushy-tailed

= phrase: alert

The behaviour of a new starter – usually short-lived.

Usage** – Jaded managers of a new employee who still has, albeit temporarily, the sunny disposition of the oh-so-very-keen-to-please interview candidate. It is also the correct Offlish response to the familiar Friday afternoon farewell:'Have a good one. See you on Monday – *bright-eyed and bushy-tailed.*'

Brownie points [§]

= n: marks of success

Credit that is rarely accepted as valid currency.

Usage** – Anxious or naive managers who cling to the belief that the office is a logical world where hard work will be justly rewarded. In the chaos of the office, the relationship between even a fair boss and his charges resembles less a finely calibrated league table of merit than a surreal game of snakes and ladders with endless permutations and no hope of a final outcome. There are no rules: points may be scored but they are just as easily lost. It is better to abstain from the game entirely.

See also **Brown-nose**

[§] The term is probably an amalgam of several usages: a 'brownie' was originally a Scottish expression for a domestic drudge; the junior branch of the Girl Guides, 'the Brownies', were named by Lady Baden-Powell after the 'brownie' elves of Scottish folklore and earned points for good deeds; while brown points were awarded for American food rationing in the second world war. The term was first recorded after the war as American army slang.

Brown-nose

= v: to behave in an obsequious manner

A proclivity demonstrated by strong-stomached individuals for those occasions when *brownie points* have proved to be insufficient.

Usage** – Disgruntled and out-of-favour managers of their (more successful) *colleagues*.

See also **Brownie points**; **Colleague**; **Puppet**

Buck, biggest bang for the
= phrase: the best return

A noisy demonstration of faith.

Usage*** – Managers who persist in the belief that using Americanisms is both smart and sophisticated.

See also **Ball, curve**; **Plate, step up to the**; **Problem**; **Z**

Buddy
= n & v: a mentor; to act as a mentor

To give a helping hand can be a very rewarding experience.

Usage*** – *Californian managers* for whom acting as *mentor* is a quasi-mystical experience and integral to their philosophy; experienced managers who have got behind with their filing and value an extra pair of hands.

See also **Californian manager**; **Mentor**

Bung
= n: a payment; a bribe

A stopgap solution.

Usage* – Thwarted *Sales managers* looking for an easy answer: 'Can we sling him a *bung* then?' *No-nonsense managers*, on the other hand, will remember the former Arsenal manager George Graham as a cautionary tale.

See also **No-nonsense manager**; **Sales manager**; **Sweetener**

Bust, shit or

= phrase: make every effort

A word of warning: the office can be a very messy environment.

Usage ** – For the *No-nonsense manager* a daily duty and a perennial programme: 'We can't take this lying down. We're nearly out of runway so it's *shit or bust* on this one, *guys*.' Just make sure you aren't the one left to clean up when things go wrong.

See also **Guys**; **No-nonsense manager**; **Omelette, you have to crack eggs to make an**

Buy in

= n & v: acceptance or agreement; to accept or agree

A gamble taken with money that belongs to someone else.

Usage *** – Managers everywhere as it is an essential part of any decision: 'We need a comfort blanket here. Have we got *buy in* from all the *key movers and shakers*?' / 'I can really *buy into* that.' For the *Californian manager* and *Training manager* it is a guiding principle.

See also **Californian manager**; **Key**; **Shaker, mover and**; **Training manager**

Buzz

= n: a humming sound; a feeling of excitement; publicity

An irritating sound wherever and whenever it is encountered.

Usage ***** – A '*motivational*' word popular with the *HR manager* that conjures pictures in the mind of electrical circuits or annoying insects and is, in fact, peculiarly demotivating: 'We need to get a *buzz* going on this one.' This may also be because it usually issues from the lips of beaming halfwits who believe that sprinkling their speech with phrases such as '*team*' and '*people*', '*commitment*' and '*passion*', will create a supercharged

Californian manager

Sincere and serious, he is an *enthusiastic* endorser of the theories of business self-help *gurus*. '*Feedback*', '*input*' and '*motivation*' are his watchwords and he prides himself on his political correctness. He enjoys solving problems and will seek '*inspiration*' from his current favourite business *mentor*: 'How would Buddha/*Sun Tzu*/Hannibal/Genghis Khan/Ernest Shackleton/*Tom Peters*/Mrs Thatcher/Kevin Keegan/Sir Clive Woodward/Natasha Bedingfield approach this?' Sometimes he may even ask this question out loud. Invariably, he will describe himself as '*empathetic*'; he encourages '*buy in*' and '*win/win*' solutions; and is likely to inquire regularly whether you are 'in a good place right now?'. Typically, he aspires to a role in Human Resources where, he believes, he can best use his '*interpersonal*' skills. He is despised by everyone and should, if at all possible, be avoided.[§]

See also **Aspirational**; **Autonomy**; **Bridges, build**; **Buddy**; **Buy in**; **Buzz**; **Change**; **Colleague**; **Collegiate**; **Culture, no blame**; **Empathy**; **Enthusiasm**; **Feedback**; **Growth, personal**; **Hearts and minds, winning**; **Holistic**; **Huddle**; **Influencer**; **Input**; **Inspirational**; **Interface**; **Interpersonal**; **Learnings**; **Lose/lose**; **Mentor**; **Motivation**; **Partnership**; **Tom Peters**; **Problem**; **Situation, no win**; **Sun Tzu**; **Surprises, policy of no**; **Win/win**; **Wow factor**

[§] The collective noun for *Californian managers* is a haze or stroke.

workforce only too willing to '*go the extra mile*' in pursuit of larger profits. It is also used by earnest *Californian managers* and by *Training managers* who have swallowed whole the Training Manual.

See also **Californian manager**; **Commitment**; **Human Resources manager**; **Mile, go the extra**; **Motivation**; **Passion**; **People**; **Training manager**

Can, left holding the
= phrase: get the blame for something

A simple game resembling *musical chairs* in reverse.

Usage*** – All managers: those who never get the prize as well as those who are regular winners.

See also **Culture, no blame**; **Musical chairs**

Cannon, loose
= n: a heterodox individual

A word of warning: the office can be a dangerous place.

Usage*** – Journalists describing an unorthodox executive at an underperforming company (by contrast, an unorthodox executive at a successful company is *'off-the-wall'*); also *Machiavellian managers* carefully planting the notion that a *colleague* is a hothead. It is a useful all-purpose slur as it rarely requires substantiation and, in most instances, the rumour will quickly solidify into a widely held belief.

See also **Machiavellian manager**; **Off-the-wall**

Card, red
= n: a card used by a referee to indicate a player has been sent off

A compulsory exit and a melancholy phrase expressing in compact form the heartbreaking transience of life.

Usage** – Via *Premiership English* it is used by senior managers on the sad fate of a former *colleague*; usually uttered in a resigned, there-but-for-the-grace-of-God tone: 'One day he's top

dog. The next it's a *red card* and the black bin-bag treatment';
also *No-nonsense managers* on the sad fate of a former
colleague, always in a brisk, well-he-had-it-coming accent: 'What
did he expect? It had to be a *red card* and his marching orders.'

See also **Feet, went in with both**; **No-nonsense manager**;
Premiership English

Card, trump
= n: a decisive advantage

To be held up one's sleeve for use in an emergency and then
winningly slapped down on the table with a flourish.

Usage** – Victorious managers; defeated managers.

Cat, fat
= n: an influential person; the head of a business

A majestic beast who, so long as he is fed well and regularly, is
reasonably benign; however, he does not like to be handled and,
when provoked, he can be extremely vicious.

Usage* – Now in widespread usage, the phrase was initially
popularised by the muckraking tabloid press as an abusive
shorthand for hard-pressed *CEOs*, many of whom are worth
every penny of their stupendous salaries. They can't be blamed,
after all, if their own board members regularly sanction huge
salary increases and the payment of annual bonuses irrespective
of the performance of the company.

See also **CEO**; **Inspirational**; **Pussycat**; **Strategy**

Catch-22
= n: any action which also brings about its negation (from
Joseph Heller's second world war novel)

An underlying principle of the office as well as in war.
Companies must increase profits to satisfy shareholders. In

order to do so they must give customers better services and lower prices, but this tends to increase costs and reduces profits. Result: the birth of Offlish to explain away the contradiction.

Usage** – Managers attempting to explain a situation they don't understand; *Ambitious managers* because they think it makes them sound more intelligent; *Thesaurus managers* as often as possible in order to display their supposed intellectual precosity.§

See also **Ambitious manager**; **Thesaurus manager**

§ If there is a chance the *Thesaurus manager* will go on to name the book, and the author, and give an outline of the central gag – Yossarian who wants to stop flying missions as it is dangerous; therefore, must be sane; therefore, must keep flying – and, if anyone is still listening, retell the anecdote in which Heller, when asked why he hadn't written another book as good as his first, replied: 'Who has?'

Challenge (from the Latin for 'a false accusation')
= n & v: an invitation to a fight or contest; to call into question

A thing to be thrown down. (A steady supply of gauntlets is required in the office.)

Usage***** – One of the most popular of all Offlish words, it is used instead of the standard English 'question' or 'observation' by managers of all kinds in discussions and *meetings* where it usually barely obscures their frustration and anger: 'I have a *challenge* . . .' / 'I'd like to *challenge* that . . .' (translation: 'You dolt. You nincompoop. You pea-brain . . .'). 'Issue' is widely used as a substitute. In addition, '*challenge*' is regularly used as a synonym for '*problem*'.

See also **Meeting**; **Opportunity**; **Problem**

Change
= v: to make different

A state that is always inconvenient.

Usage **** – An Offlish word with exceptional pliancy, it is used by managers everywhere – from the Chairman to the humblest tyro – especially when defending an unpopular decision. It is a watchword for the *Training manager* and the *Californian manager* in relation to *personal growth*, and it also occurs frequently in job adverts for senior positions: 'You will be able to gain the trust and confidence of the business. You will galvanise people and be a champion of *change*.' Substitute phrases are '*sea change*', 'deep change' and, most absurdly, 'transformational change'. And '*change*', in case there was any doubt, is brought about by 'change agents'.

See also **Californian manager**; **Growth, personal**; **Training manager**

Change, sea
= n: a profound alteration or modification

The kind of *change* that results in a different situation than before.

Usage **** – A beautiful Shakespearean coinage[§] now widely and blandly used as a synonym for any kind of new circumstances.

See also **Change**; **Change, step**; **Paradigm shift**

[§] Ariel's song from *The Tempest* 1:2: 396–401:

> Full fathom five thy father lies;
> Of his bones are coral made;
> Those are pearls that were his eyes;
> Nothing of him that doth fade
> But doth suffer a *sea-change*
> Into something rich and strange.

Change, step
= n: a profound alteration or modification

A popular Offlish dance movement based on the one step forwards, one step backwards formula.

Usage***** – *CEOs* lazily inflating a point; self-important managers lazily inflating a point; managers drawing attention to their supposed achievements. Also in job adverts for senior positions: 'You will have demonstrated a *track record* of over-achievement, commercial focus and collaboration within the business to shape people, processes and solutions that have brought about organisational *step change*' (translation: 'Blah, blah, blah . . .').

See also **Ambitious manager**; **Change**; **Change, sea**; **CEO**; **Paradigm shift**; **Track record**

Charlatan (from the Italian 'to babble')[§]
= n: an untrustworthy person; a mountebank

A storyteller of exceptional ability.

Usage* – Managers of a (more successful) *colleague* whom they dislike.

See also **Colleague**; **Guru**; **Inspirational**

[§] It was the economist J. K. Galbraith who wisely said that 'people only use the word *guru* because *charlatan* is too long'.

Cheese, big
= n: an influential person

A *player*.

Usage** – Directors with a wary respect for a business opponent; deferential managers.

See also **Bigwig**; **Fromage, grand**; **Hitter, big**; **Heavyweight**; **Player**

Chest, war
= n: a treasury

A useful item of office furniture, the keys to which

must be guarded very carefully.

Usage [**] – Journalists reporting on rumours of a takeover bid; canny *Finance managers* who, in an emergency, know where to locate additional funds; *Samurai managers* for whom the military connotations are too tempting to ignore.

See also **Finance manager**; **Samurai manager**

Chief Executive Officer (CEO)

Charismatic, narcissistic, easily bored; an exceptionally intelligent and capable man (occasionally a woman) of many and diverse talents. Omnipresent and omniscient – like God he makes his presence felt everywhere. Sometimes a strong leader and brave strategist; sometimes a figurehead and *mentor*. Sometimes a skilled politician; sometimes a *maverick*; always hugely wealthy. His only needs are lots of free time to think; slavish obedience; a massive office; a PA willing to lay down their life; huge annual bonuses and a too-big-to-count-if-he-lives-to-be-a-hundred pension. A *player* who is feared by everyone, courted by many, he should, if at all possible, be avoided. [§]

See also **Aligned**; **Balls**; **Box, thinking outside the**; **Cat, fat**; **Change, step**; **Collegiate**; **Community**; **Consumer agenda**; **Core**; **Correct!**; **Customer-facing**; **Days, bad old**; **Dinosaur**; **Downsize**; **Duck, lame**; **Flip side**; **Floor, back to the**; **Food chain**; **Fresh air, breath of**; **Go for it!**; **Hero-to-zero**; **Hindsight**; **Jigsaw, final piece of the**; **Knockout blow**; **Maverick**; **Mentor**; **Mercurial**; **Midas touch**; **Non-core**; **Own**; **Player**; **Professional, consummate**; **Restructure**; **Strategy**; **Talent, pool of**; **Team, dream**; **Tweak**; **World, brave new**; **World-class**

[§] The collective noun for *CEOs* is a wad.

Chin, take it on the

= phrase: acceptance of punishment or ill luck

A stoical response to a blow that is often unprovoked and undeserved.

Usage ** – Resigned managers inured to the rough-and-tumble of the office.

Cigar, close but no

= phrase: almost correct or successful

There are no second prizes in the office.

Usage *** – Humourless managers putting down an underling in a *meeting*.

See also **Humour, sense of**; **Meeting**

Class, different

= phrase: demonstrating excellence

A high accolade.

Usage * – A *No-nonsense manager* using *Premiership English* to compliment a workmate – or himself: 'I was *different class*, I was.'

See also **No-nonsense manager**; **Premiership English**

Cloud-cuckoo-land

= n: a fanciful or ideal place (from Aristophanes's *The Birds* – a city built in the air)

Unsurprisingly, a popular haunt, as the people there are perennially friendly and life harmonious. Why would anyone want to leave when everything is so perfect?

Usage *** – Tabloid journalists of out-of-touch executives; also out-of-sorts managers of anyone who disagrees with them:

'Do me a favour! What's he on! He's barking up the wrong tree again. He's in *cloud-cuckoo-land* if he thinks that . . .' and so on and so on.

Clout
= n: influence; a blow

An invisible though highly effective weapon.

Usage** – Managers lamenting their lowly place in the hierarchy: 'I want to *make it happen*, I just don't have the *clout* . . .'

See also **Food chain**; **Happen, make it**

Coal face, at the
= phrase: where work is done

A situation that precludes effective cogitation.

Usage** – *Sales managers* (and sales personnel) repeatedly as they believe that because they occasionally speak to customers (when there is no other choice) they are the only people who really know what is happening in the company: 'Here we are busting a gut on a daily basis. If they got off their fat backsides and spent some time *at the coal face* and got their hands dirty, they'd soon see *what's what*.'

See also **Eyes and ears**; **Sales manager**; **Sharp end, at the**; **What's what**

Cocks on the block
= phrase: demonstrate mettle

A proud gesture.

Usage*** – In an emergency, an ultimatum laid down to his *team*, irrespective of their gender, by the *No-nonsense manager*: 'It's time to deliver, *guys*. It's *cocks on the block* time.' Similarly, it is used by *Sales managers* as an injunction to their *team* to deliver the budgeted figures irrespective of their personal feelings as to the realism of the forecast: *'Cocks on the blocks*, chaps. It's a *JFDI!* situation.'

See also **Guys**; **JFDI!**; **No-nonsense manager**; **Sales manager**; **Team**

Cock-up
= n: a muddle

Occasionally a personal error, but more often the result of the involvement of two or more people acting together.

Usage** – Embittered managers, who *know* that they could do better, describing another corporate gaffe or trashing a *colleague*: 'It was a right *cock-up* because of that clown.'

See also **Colleague**; **Conspiracy**

Cojones
= n: courage (pronounced 'co-honayes', from the Spanish for testicles)

Often claimed to be a necessary attribute for all successful men (and women).

Usage** – Managers, especially *No-nonsense managers*, who have seen too many Hollywood action films.

See also **Ballbreaker**; **Balls**

Cold, catch a
= phrase: a mishap

A common occurrence and a constant worry.

Usage*** – *No-nonsense managers*: 'I want every *box ticked*, mind you – we don't want to *catch a cold* on this one.'

See also **No-nonsense manager**; **Tick in the box**

Colleague

= n: a workmate

An ally, collaborator, companion and team-mate.§

Usage**** – Managers everywhere speaking formally (that is, anywhere where they might be overheard); cynical *HR managers* speaking ironically (that is, anywhere where they will *not* be overheard); also naive *Training managers* and *Californian managers* habitually.

See also **Action; Ambition; Anorak; Appropriate; Bag of snakes, mad as a; Ballbreaker; Banana skin; Bean counter; Brown-nose; Californian manager; Cannon, loose; Charlatan; Cock-up; Stephen R Covey; Cupboard, skeletons in the; Curve, learning; Dead horse, flogging a; Freak, control; Go, let; Goal, own; Hackneyed; Heads up; Hero-to-zero; High-flier; Human Resources manager; Jerry-built; Journeyman; Liar; Loser; Mentor; Midas touch; Muppet; Nerd; Networker; Niche, carve out a; Off-brand; Order of the boot; Plot, lose the; Pipedream; Plate, enough on one's; Puppet; Shambles; Shoot oneself in the foot; Snake in the grass; Space cadet; Square peg in a round hole; Story, sob; Sucker; Swing bin, mad as a; Training manager; When you are in a hole stop digging; Yes-man**

§ It was Don Corleone who wisely said: 'Keep your friends close but your enemies closer.'

Collegiate

= adj: resembling a college

A fabled style of united collaboration.

Usage** – *CEOs* sending a message to the press about the unity of the board: 'It's a *collegiate* approach with a strong *team* spirit'; cynical *HR directors* presenting utopian plans for organisational *change* that merely represents a degree of tinkering with the existing *command and control* model of management. Also earnest *Californian managers* describing their own management style: 'I'm into a *collegiate vision* kind of approach.'

See also **Change**; **CEO**; **Control, command and**; **Guys**; **Team**;
Vision

Colours
= n: commitment; beliefs

Often nailed circumspectly to the nearest fence.

Usage** – *CEO*s exhorting the '*troops*' at the annual conference:
'We need to show our true *colours* in the months ahead';
Samurai managers demanding unswerving loyalty: 'Get those
colours nailed to the mast . . .'

See also **CEO**; **Samurai manager**; **Sit on the fence**; **Troops, the**

Comics, reading too many
= phrase: fantastical disposition

Behold the boy; behold the man.

Usage** – A phrase via *Premiership English* (originally created
by *Ron Atkinson*) and popular with *No-nonsense managers*:
'This'll never fly, will it? He's been *reading too many comics*,
he has.' This is the office equivalent of attempting to chip the
big German keeper from 35 yards in a swirling wind with
seconds to go and needing a goal to get you through with
your centre forward screaming for the ball in space on the
penalty spot.

See also **Ron Atkinson**; **No-nonsense manager**; **Premiership
English**

Commercially minded
= adj: from a commercial point of view

A mongrel term: the offspring of fashion and inanity.

Usage**** – Unblushing executives who don't care if they are talking nonsense; pretentious, jargon-ridden job adverts written by empty-headed *HR managers*; eager-to-please candidates who hope that Offlish will make them appear in-the-club, business-like, pliant and, therefore, suitable for corporate employment; on-the-make managers who use Offlish gobbledegook to show their seeming *commitment* to the cause; lazy managers who take refuge in Offlish rather than thinking for themselves; also *Unironic managers* who don't know any better.

See also **Human Resources manager**; **Unironic manager**

Commitment
= n: a declared attachment to a cause; loyalty; devotion

A trait that is highly regarded. It is merely coincidental that it is also related to the word for an order to be sent to prison.

Usage ***** – Formerly companies asked for loyalty and in return the worker was guaranteed a job for life and a career *ladder* to climb rung by rung, year by year. Now companies ask for unwavering *commitment* and in return the worker is guaranteed incessant organisational *change*, and the likelihood that he will, at some point, be made redundant irrespective of his experience or competency.

See also **Action-oriented**; **Ante**; **Change**; **Energy, high levels of**; **Enthusiasm**; **Hungry manager**; **Ladder**; **Out, up or**; **Passion**; **Tom Peters**; **Restructure**

Community
= n: a body of persons in the same locality

Increasingly these are of the gated variety – presumably in order to keep people out.

Usage **** – This is the result of a new form of *restructuring*. Recently some companies have dispensed with departments and have instituted *communities* in their place. This change in nomenclature is meant to indicate a move towards self-determination, humane values and flexible communication within the organisation but, oddly, is always at the behest of the parent company, imposed by the board or as a response to a study commissioned from *management consultants*. It is used most frequently by *CEOs* with a God-complex.

See also **CEO**; **Management consultant**; **Restructure**

Competitive advantage
= n: to secure an improved position in the marketplace

A heartfelt prayer to the God of the Market.

Usage ***** – Everyone from the Chairman to the most junior manager to encapsulate the supposed benefits of anything from the grandest company *strategy* to the humblest departmental wheeze; also job adverts for senior positions: 'The role is about increasing shareholder value via identifying improvement *opportunities* and instigating programmes for delivering *competitive advantage*.'

See also **Opportunity**; **Strategy**

Conspiracy
= n: a plot; secret plan

A tried-and-trusted method for decision-making that has been effective for centuries.

Usage * – A central principle for the *Machiavellian manager*, it is used most often by paranoid managers who have found themselves 'out of the loop'.

See also **Cock-up**; **Machiavellian manager**

Consumer agenda
= n: what people want

Your guess is as good as anybody's. Confidence is everything.

Usage *** – *CEOs* explaining the company's *strategy* to the City: 'We aim to be an organisation *driven* by the dynamics of the *consumer agenda*'; *Marketing managers*, occasionally even using statistics and facts, to state the fashionably obvious. It is also useful to the *Ambitious manager* as its haziness makes it almost unchallengeable.

See also **Ambitious manager**; **CEO**; **Drive**; **Marketing manager**; **Strategy**

Consumer-driven

= adj: following the needs of the consumer

A mongrel term: the offspring of fashion and cant.

Usage **** – Sardonic *management consultants*; unblushing executives who don't care if they are talking nonsense; pretentious, jargon-ridden job adverts written by empty-headed *HR managers*; eager-to-please candidates who hope that Offlish will make them appear in-the-club, businesslike, pliant and, therefore, suitable for corporate employment; on-the-make managers who use Offlish gobbledegook to show their seeming *commitment* to the cause; lazy managers who take refuge in Offlish rather than thinking for themselves; also *Unironic managers* who don't know any better. (A phrase sometimes used as a substitute is 'customer-intuitive'.)

See also **Commitment**; **Human Resources manager**; **Management consultant**; **Unironic manager**

Contribution

= n: something added to a shared cause

Always valued.

Usage ** – Executives and *Unironic managers* of people who have left the business; *Training managers* in training sessions.

See also **Go, let**; **Training manager**; **Unironic manager**

Control, command and
= phrase: centralised decision-making

A style of management that is much derided, usually described as out of date, yet which remains the standard model for companies everywhere.

Usage *** – Disgruntled managers who want to be in control and issuing the commands.

See also **Collegiate**

Cool!
= interj: excellent

A ubiquitous expression of approval; however, its use is inadvisable once over 25 years of age.

Usage **** – Experienced managers everywhere forgetting or ignoring their years.

Core
= n & adj: the centre; the essential

Like an onion a company has many layers.

Usage *** – Whenever a company has to announce poor *results* the *CEO* will inevitably announce that they are reviewing the *strategy* to assess which 'areas'/'competencies'/'drivers'/'levers' are '*core*' and '*non-core*'. A '*back to basics*' programme 'to get us back on our feet again' is the inevitable result of the review. A frequently used substitute is '*key*'.

See also **Basics, back to**; **Bread and butter**; **CEO**; **Key**; **Non-core**; **Principles, first**; **Results**; **Strategy**

Corn, earn one's
= phrase: justify one's salary

Always check the small print of any employment contract.

Usage* – Via *Premiership English* where, for reasons no one understands, it is applied exclusively to instances of brave goalkeeping where a vital stop saves a point or 'keeps his side in the match'. In the office the goalkeeper becomes a junior manager, and the commentator his condescending boss: 'He really *earned his corn* with that deal, he did.'

See also **Premiership English**

Correct!
= interj: accurate; an expression of approval

A word that requires a crisp intonation and an exclamation mark to be fully effective!

Usage*** – A patronising acknowledgement from a superior to a junior of a point properly argued in a debate or *meeting*. Here the politics of a particular situation are dramatically uncovered: the master and the servant are revealed in their allotted roles. It is used by *CEOs* to their directors; directors to their senior managers; managers to their junior managers; and by junior managers to their minions.

See also **CEO**; **Meeting**; **Order, pecking**

Cost-effective
= adj: producing the most profit

An underlying principle of good business practice that is the cause of many arguments and disputes. Like a kaleidoscope, a shift in perspective produces a completely different picture; or, as the old saying has it: 'There are many ways to skin a cat.'

Usage** – A term, usually a question, that is used in a wide variety of circumstances where a piece of work has to be evaluated financially. It is used obsessively by *Finance managers* for whom time really *is* money. As it is virtually meaningless without elaboration, it is a useful question for the *Ambitious manager* to ask in a *meeting* because, more often than not, no one will object and he knows that he will appear both interested and moderately informed.

See also **Ambitious manager**; **Finance manager**; **Meeting**

Covey, Stephen R.

Inspirational American business *guru* responsible for the bestselling – 'Over 10 Million Copies Sold' – The 7 Habits of Highly Effective People: Powerful Lessons in Personal *Change*, in which he presents 'a *holistic*, integrated, principle-centred approach for solving personal and professional problems'.

The seven essential habits are:

1) Be *proactive*
2) Begin with the end in mind
3) Put first things first
4) Think *win/win*
5) Seek first to understand then be understood
6) *Synergize*
7) Sharpen the saw

The book is dedicated 'To my *colleagues, empowered* and *empowering*'.

See also **Change**; **Colleague**; **Empower**; **Guru**; **Holistic**; **Inspirational**; **Proactive**; **Synergy**; **Win/win**

CrackBerry
= n: a person who obsessively uses their BlackBerry

An up-to-the-minute ailment.

Usage *** – Despondent, put-upon subordinates who know that

their boss can issue commands from anywhere and at any time: 'He's a *control freak*. A *CrackBerry*. Doesn't he sleep? Doesn't he realise that I sleep?'

See also **Always-on**; **Freak, control**; **Full-on**; **Hungry manager**

Cracks, fall down the
= phrase: to be lost

A common accident.

Usage *** – A euphemism used by worried managers who have to report lack of progress or a failure: 'We didn't *drop the ball* exactly. It just seemed to, well, *fall down the cracks* . . .' (translation: 'It wasn't me. It wasn't my fault. It was him. It was them').

See also **Ball, dropped the**

Cracks, papering over the
= phrase: to obliterate the evidence

A time-consuming, laborious process and a vital managerial skill.

Usage * – Managers reflecting privately on the outcome of one of the company's *strategic* initiatives; also journalists judging the effectiveness of a *strategic* initiative.

See also **Strategy**

Critical path
= n: the stages in a process or operation

Often poorly signposted.

Usage **** – A planning tool that is a nagging obsession for the *IT manager*: 'How are we *impacting* on the *critical path*?'; for everyone else it is a document wholly divorced from reality. It is also used by managers wanting to add a patina of pseudoscientific authority to a presentation or argument.

See also **IT manager**; **Impact**

Crown jewels
= n: a monarch's formal jewellery

Valuable historical items and, therefore, a useful source of cash in an emergency.

Usage*** – Journalists who recognise that the company is about to 'go down the plughole' (or is 'circling the drain') pointing to a forthcoming disastrous crash: '. . . once the *crown jewels* have been sold off, it won't be long before they are down to the bare bones'; also experienced managers who think the company is 'being sold down the river'. By contrast, *No-nonsense managers* will only use the phrase as lewd slang.

See also **No-nonsense manager**; **U-turn**

Culture, no blame
= phrase: free of recrimination and condemnation

An admirable stance, but unsustainable when something goes wrong.

Usage**** – Rueful managers '*left holding the can*'; also *Californian managers* for whom it is an important doctrine: 'I'm really into dialogue and a *no blame culture* kind of approach.'

See also **Californian manager**; **Can, left holding the**

Cupboard, skeletons in the
= phrase: damaging secrets

Some offices resemble a well-stocked crypt. Be careful which doors you choose to open.

Usage*** – Journalists probing the official corporate history; managers speculating about the career history of one of their *colleagues*.

See also **Colleague**; **CV**

Curlies, short and

= phrase: pubic hair

Always a provocation in the office.

Usage** – *Sales managers* routinely:'Let's go for the kill on this one. I want these *guys* by the *short and curlies*, begging for their lives.'

See also **Guys**; **Sales manager**

CV

= n: curriculum vitae – a summary of a person's education and achievements

A short biographical outline designed to demonstrate one's worthiness for employment – sometimes (as the course of life rarely runs smooth) accurate

Usage* – In job adverts:'Your *CV* will show a proven *track record* of success.'There are, of course, a plethora of books setting out in exhaustive details how best to complete such a document in order to achieve the desired result.All of them instruct the candidate to tell the truth and nothing but the truth.This is coward's advice.A judicious twist here and there of the facts is the most sensible and practical advice. Delivered confidently, the majority of exaggerations are rarely detectable in interviews. Simply avoid the difficult-to-carry-off whoppers such as speaking several languages fluently; having written a bestselling novel; being a Duke, Earl or Lord. Most interviewers are so tired, self-absorbed or plain incompetent that the chances of being rumbled are small. It is also important to set out into the sea of corporate life with the correct attitude.

See also **Ambassador**; **Cupboard, skeletons in the**; **Self-starter**; **Track record**; **Versatile**

Curve, learning

= n: the rate at which a new skill is acquired

Invariably steep.

Usage** – *Unironic managers* routinely; managers in a new role foolishly admitting to difficulties; managers lipsmackingly revelling in a new *colleague*'s inadequacies.

See also **Colleague**; **Unironic manager**

Custodian
= n: a guardian

A very, very important position.

Usage** – A posh word used to inflate the importance of a particular task or responsibility by managers everywhere who require a linguistic embellishment to bring dignity to the drudgery of the daily round. It is an especial favourite of the *Brand manager* who will routinely describe himself as the '*custodian* of the *brand*'. Whenever you hear the word, and if you have confidence that your position in the company is unimpeachable – or if you don't give a flying fig – then it is worth responding with the Juvenal epigram: 'Quis custodiet ipsos custodes?'[§] This will secure you an instant reputation either as a fearsome intellectual not to be trifled with or as a troublesome egghead who is better off in a university library. What is there to lose?

See also **Brand**; **Brand manager**

[§] From Juvenal's Epigrams VI: 'Who will guard the guards themselves?'

Customer behaviour, changing
= phrase: bringing about a change in people

Harder than it seems: successful examples would include the invention of the wheel, Buddha, Christ, the Black Death, democracy, Winston Churchill and the contraceptive pill.

Usage*** – Often cited as the principle underlying a corporate *strategy*, it is used by *Marketing managers* who know that the exercise is doomed but have to play along to retain their jobs.

See also **Marketing manager**; **Paradigm shift**; **Strategy**; **Wheel, reinvent the**

Customer-facing
= adj: dealing with customers

An invidious position. As the old song has it, 'Smile, though your heart is breaking.'

Usage **** – This is a clumsy term that is usually indicative of some kind of corporate crisis. After all, no one would willingly talk about the needs and wants of customers. It is used by *Sales* and *Marketing directors* when making self-serving *strategy* presentations and *CEOs* when announcing a '*back to basics*' programme to the City after a poor set of financial results: '*Going forward* our aim is to be a *customer-facing* organisation.' Similar, but slightly less common, phrases are 'customer/consumer/client obsessed/focused/oriented'; or 'close to the customer' or 'customer first'. It is often used in job adverts, especially for sales and marketing positions: 'Only those who are customer-centric should apply'/'You will have the opportunity to *drive* significant *change* and business growth through customer-focused innovation'/'Absolute customer orientation for the purpose of optimum customer satisfaction will characterize your plan of action' and so on and so on.

See also **Basics, back to**; **Change**; **CEO**; **Drive**; **Forward, going**; **Marketing manager**; **Sales manager**; **Strategy**

Customer is always right, the
= phrase: the customer is always right

A maxim without universal validity that a *small* number of companies have made the basis of their success.

Usage ***** – *Unironic managers* whose belief in the clichés and calloused phrases of Offlish is thoroughgoing; managers who wish to deflect criticism from an unpopular decision; also toadying managers reiterating the company mantra.

See also **Unironic manager**

Days, bad old
= phrase: an unfortunate period in the past

Formerly known as the golden age.

Usage*** – A new *CEO* assuring the world-at-large that there are 'good times ahead'; piqued long-serving managers who believe that the company is being led inexorably to disaster.

See also **CEO; Days, halcyon**

Days, halcyon
= phrase: a time of happiness and calm

Always in the past.

Usage* – *Worldly-wise managers* reflecting on bygone (and entirely fictitious) achievements. An ironic interjection such as 'Ah, yes, where are the snows of yesteryear?' will be met with a kindly nod and a rheumy eye.

See also **Worldly-wise manager**

Dead horse, flogging a
= phrase: useless activity

A distasteful and exhausting task – a commonplace in the office.

Usage**** – Managers commenting on a *colleague*'s misjudgement.

See also **Colleague; Commitment**

Defenestration
= n: the act of throwing something or someone out of a window

A word of warning: the office can be a dangerous place.

Usage* – *Thesaurus managers* reflecting on another boardroom departure.

See also **Restructure**; **Thesaurus manager**

DNA
= n: genetic composition

The essence of a company that should not be tampered with.

Usage** – *Thesaurus managers*, as well as pompous executives who know nothing about deoxyribonucleic acid but have skimmed enough magazine articles to know that the term will enable them to appear just a little bit more up to date than their peers: '*Blue-sky thinking* is the *DNA* of this company.'

See also **Thesaurus manager**; **Thinking, blue-sky**

Devil and the deep blue sea, between the
= proverb: a choice between equally disadvantageous alternatives

A familiar dilemma in the office.

Usage* – Resigned managers.

See also **Catch-22**; **Hobson's Choice**; **Rock and a hard place, between a**

Dickswinging
= adj: swaggeringly arrogant

A déclassé term for a *player*.

Usage** – A *No-nonsense manager* paying due deference to the great man (or woman).

See also **No-nonsense manager**; **Player**

Difference, making a

= phrase: having an important influence or effect

An intervention that occasionally produces a positive outcome.

Usage **** – A noble aim espoused by the naive or enshrined in *mission statements* and mechanically repeated by the board at every opportunity; job adverts, especially for *people* positions; keen young candidates at interviews; also *Californian managers* and *Training managers* routinely.

See also **Californian manager**; **Entrepreneur**; **Mission statement**; **People**; **Training manager**

Dilbert

A highly respected cultural commentator, business theorist and creator of the 'Dilbert Principle': 'The most ineffective workers are systematically moved to the place where they can do the least damage – management.'

Dinosaur

= n: an extinct reptile; a useless person

In the office there is a place for everyone.

Usage ** – Managers of ageing and unsuccessful *CEOs* (by contrast, successful ageing *CEOs* are 'experienced' and 'respected') and disaffected younger managers of their ageing superiors: 'He's been here for far too long' (translation: 'When can I have his job, salary, car, office, pension, secretary, perks?').

See also **CEO**

Direction, strategic

= phrase: plan of action

A journey that only makes sense retrospectively.

Usage *** – Cynical Chairmen habitually: 'The road ahead will be hard but, united, we can achieve our goal. Our *strategic direction* is clear. Our purpose firm' (translation: '. . . but let's keep our options open, shall we?').

See also **Game, name of the**; **Plan**; **Strategy**

Directionally
= adv: indicating the direction something might take

A form of muted applause that may easily segue into catcalls.§

Usage*** – Cagey directors and canny managers who are alert to political undercurrents: 'It's not there yet . . . but it's right *directionally* . . .' It is a word that would not have been found in any dictionary created even five years ago, which has become popular as it does not commit the user to a clear opinion. It is ideal, therefore, for expressing a view, thereby making a mark, while sufficiently insubstantial that it can be withdrawn or amended so as not to lose face.

§ A performance perfected, for example, by Statler and Waldorf from the Muppets.

Disconnect
= v & n: to detach; a breakdown

A rupture in the natural order.

Usage ***** – A good verb widely used as a bad noun to signify that a process in the corporate body is not working effectively: 'There's a bit of a *disconnect* here.' It can become so popular with the perpetrator that it becomes synonymous with anything that doesn't happen as expected: 'I ordered a latte not a cappuccino. There must be a *disconnect* with the barista'/ 'This was in my diary for tomorrow. There must be a *disconnect* with my PA' and so on and so on.

See also **Left hand not knowing what the right hand is doing**

Dive, deep
= phrase: a detailed review

A dangerous enterprise that should be undertaken only by professionals.

Usage**** – Senior managers who have heard other senior managers use the phrase: 'We should look to do a number on this one. A *deep dive* session could present *learnings* for opportunities *going forward*. We need to get really *granular* here.'

See also **Drains-up, we need to pull up the manhole cover and have a; Forward, going; Granular; Learnings**

Diving, ducking and
= phrase: evasive action

An effective means of self-protection.

Usage** – Naive managers who have been wholly outmanoeuvred by their more politically astute workmates. The influence of the noble art of boxing in the office has long been underestimated.

See also **Knockout blow; Ropes, on the**

Doable
= adj: achievable

Commonly posed as a very important question.

Usage**** – Thrusting executives and senior managers everywhere: 'So, talking broad brush, is this *doable* then?' Once defined by dictionaries as rare, this is now an Offlish commonplace.

Dog, working like a
= phrase: exceptionally industrious

A state of self-pity brought about by a period of sustained heroic achievement that has gone unrecognised and unrewarded.

Usage** – Managers, with a what-can-I-do grimace: 'I'd love to help but I'm snowed under at the moment. I'm *working like a dog* here' (translation: 'Why don't you go and take a flying leap?'). It is useful in the office to have a supply of 'working like a ...' analogies.

See also **Navvy, working like a**; **Ride, bumpy**; **Stakhanovite, working like a**; **Trojan, working like a**

Dog's bollocks, the
= phrase: the best; the finest

A considered and generous accolade.

Usage** – *No-nonsense managers* expressing unrestricted admiration: 'That's the *dog's bollocks*, that is.'

See also **No-nonsense manager**

Doh!
= interj: an expostulation (popularised by Homer Simpson)

For maximum effect this must be accompanied by a smack of the palm against the forehead.

Usage*** – Humourless managers confessing to a minor mistake or misunderstanding.

See also **Humour, sense of**

Doomsday scenario
= n: the worst possible conclusion

A story with a single outcome but that can be read in many different ways.

Usage*** – Executives, privately, expecting the worst; *Dramatic managers* envisaging death, tragedy or ruin – again; *Machiavellian managers* spreading panic; *Sales managers* foreseeing a missed bonus; *Unironic managers* fearing an unfavourable situation.

See also **Armageddon**; **Dramatic manager**; **Machiavellian manager**; **Sales manager**; **Unironic manager**

Door, knocking on the
= phrase: fit for promotion

Almost always an unwelcome intrusion.

Usage*** – Senior managers recommending a protégé: 'He's the bee's knees. The sky's the limit for him. He's certainly *knocking on the door*' (translation: 'I taught him everything he knows'). The brisk rat-a-tat-tat of the *Ambitious manager* is a regular annoyance to those earnestly, and sensibly, pursuing the quiet life.

See also **Ambitious manager**; **Mentor**

Door, open
= n: unrestricted access

A substantial barrier to communication.

Usage*** – The director's/senior manager's door is often open – on an empty office. The daily round of *meeting* after *meeting*, occasional conferences, regular away days, strategy fests and corporate junkets ('jollies') means that he is difficult to locate, let alone talk with. And when he is in the office, it is the principal task of his PA to fend off any unplanned or unwelcome visitors. The phrase is used by directors/senior managers who want to be seen as *inspirational*. The invitation is usually said with a grin and a horrible matey tone: 'You know that my *door* is always *open*' (translation: '... but if you could make an appointment, or talk to someone else, or just keep it under your *hat*, or better still, just forget about it, I'd be hugely grateful').

See also **Hat**; **Inspirational**; **Meeting**; **Street, two-way**

Door, pushing at an open
= phrase: pointless activity

A foolish error likely to result in an embarrassing tumble.

Usage ** – Supercilious managers adopting the latest vogue phrase to demonstrate that they are up-to-the-minute and in-the-know (while everyone else is out of date and out on a limb): 'Really, you're *pushing at an open door* on this one. It's already done and dusted'; also senior managers underlining a junior colleague's gaffe or, in a negotiation, pointing out the other side's childish reasoning.

See also **Feet, went in with both**

Doors, early
= phrase: at an early stage

Indisputably the best time to *set out one's stall*.

Usage ** – A phrase that has crossed over from *Premiership English* (was it, perhaps, coined by the redoubtable *Ron Atkinson*?) into Offlish and is almost meaningless in both contexts: 'We must make progress *early doors* on this.'

See also **Ron Atkinson**; **Premiership English**; **Stall, set out one's**

Downscale
= v: to reduce resources

A decision that is often pregnant with political tensions.

Usage ** – Senior managers and executives in response to criticism of a particular piece of work: 'We're having to *down-scale* our efforts on this one' (translation: 'I have hopelessly overestimated the amount of time/people/money required for this and now I am desperately back-pedalling in order to reduce our exposure in time/people/money in order to prevent this turning into a complete disaster').

See also **Upscale**

Downshift
= v: to change career in order to improve one's quality of life

A daydream: to allow the mind to drift is one of life's greatest pleasures.

Usage*** – Exhausted managers dreaming of an alternative life – making cheese or running a smallholding or writing children's novels in a converted barn in a small rural hamlet in an undiscovered area of Provence with a sea view surrounded by happy children, agreeable neighbours and gambolling animals . . .

See also **Pipedream**; **Work-life balance**

Downside
= n: a negative aspect of a situation

A pessimistic assessment that is always a cause for lamentation.

Usage*** – Nervous managers with '*bad news*' to impart.

See also **News, bad**; **Upside**

Downsize
= v: to reduce the size of an organisation; to make redundancies

A conjuring trick played on unwilling victims.

Usage**** – The process of making redundancies in order to reduce costs in a business has produced a substantial array of Offlish euphemisms.§ *Downsize* is one of the most popular. It is used by *CEOs* and executives aiming to bolster share prices by defending job cuts as a *strategy* to introduce 'flatter' management structures where the company is 'leaner and fitter', and where the whole workforce is 'closer to the customer'.

See also **Asset**; **CEO**; **Customer-facing**; **Go, let**; **Losses, cut**; **People**; **Restructure**; **Strategy**; **Synergy**; **Talent, pool of**; **Wood, dead**

§ Examples include 'consolidation', 'delayering', 're-engineering', 'reorganising', 'resource optimisation', 'retrenchment', 'rightsizing', 'smartsizing', 'streamlining'. In the tabloid press it may be described as 'getting rid of the *dead wood*', 'trimming the fat' or a 'slash and burn' exercise.

Draconian
= adj: unjustly harsh (after Draco, a lawmaker in Greece in the 7th century BC)

An uncompromising outlook. Severe situations often require severe solutions.

Usage * – *Thesaurus managers* eager to show off the depth of their historical learning. Any supplementary question will quickly unearth that their knowledge has been gleaned from a Schott's-style compilation or crossword answer.

See also **Thesaurus manager**

Drains-up, pull up the manhole cover and have a
= phrase: to investigate thoroughly

Take care: the office can be a very messy environment.

Usage ***** – *Management consultants* reflecting on the scale of the task: 'This is a *drains-up* situation that may require open-heart surgery. We need to get *granular*.' Also *Unironic managers* recommending a detailed examination of a *problem*; and *Ambitious managers* who have heard other senior managers use this asinine phrase.

See also **Ambitious manager**; **Dive, deep**; **Drill down**; **Granular**; **Management consultant**; **Problem**; **Unironic manager**

Drill down

= v: to go into detail

A muscular investigation.

Usage **** – Managers everywhere examining '*the numbers*',
but especially *Finance managers* for whom there is no greater
pleasure. It can also be used as a hideous noun: 'Could you *ping*
me the *drill-down* on those *numbers*?'

See also **Drains-up, pull up the manhole cover and have a**;
Finance manager; **Granular**; **Numbers, the**; **Ping**

Drive

= v: to be responsible; to take action; vigorous effort

An apology for egotism and misanthropy.

Usage ***** – A popular word in the Offlish vocabulary that is
used regularly in *meetings* – instead of the standard English 'do' –
where bullying is institutionalised in the name of allocating
responsibilities. It is also a favourite with jargon-spewing
management consultants as well as *Ambitious managers*
(faking interest as usual) and *Unironic managers* who are all

Offlish devotees:'You need to *drive* this!'/'Who's *driving* this one?' It is also used in job adverts for senior positions:'You will be a strong *networker* with powerful *influencing* skills to *drive change* and achieve a wide *strategic impact*' (translation:'We are in big, big trouble. Are you, by chance, a miracle worker?'). '*Action*','*land*','*nail*' and '*own*' have similar meanings and are widely used as substitutes.

See also **Action**; **Ambitious manager**; **Change**; **Impact**; **Influencer**; **Land**; **Management consultant**; **Meeting**; **Nail**; **Networker**; **Own**; **Sales manager**; **Strategy**; **Unironic manager**

Drum, bang the
= phrase: to demonstrate enthusiasm; gain support

A performance often given by the unmusical.

Usage *** – Percussive *Sales managers*, to drown out the comments of their more able and intelligent colleagues:'Listen up. We need to *bang the drum* on this one and get a *buzz* going.'

See also **Buzz**; **Sales manager**

Duck, lame
= n: a weak person

A bird occasionally sighted in the boardroom.

Usage * – Whispering managers of a *CEO* or executive who has presided over a run of poor figures amid rumours that the shareholders favour a 'makeover' at the top or even a full-scale 'regime change'.

See also **CEO**

Ducks in a row
= phrase: preparedness; show of unity

A delightful, if rare, sight.

Usage ***** – A popular, if somewhat obscure, phrase: '*Guys*, we really need to get our *ducks in a row* on this one.' The phrase probably derives from the uplifting sight of ducks flying in formation, but may have gained added currency from the now retro-fashionable sets of ceramic duck ornaments or from the popularity of plastic bright yellow children's bathroom toys. In any event, it is used by anxious managers seeking to impress upon their *team* that no mistakes will be tolerated and that everything must be in order. It is likely that they will go on to suggest that they must be 'on the same page' with 'all the *boxes ticked*' and, most importantly, '*singing from the same hymn sheet*'.

See also **Guys**; **Hymn sheet, singing from the same**; **Team**; **Thinking, joined-up**; **Tick in the box**

Easy tiger!
= interj: whoa!

A remonstrance that is only truly effective when accompanied by a palm-out gesture.

Usage ** – It is an example of acceptable corporate humour and, therefore, used by humourless managers everywhere. It is usually directed at someone in a *meeting* – for example, where someone has made a risqué joke (translation: 'Stop! You are embarrassing yourself and everybody in the room') – or where someone has shown the beginnings of a bizarre and unwarranted show of temper (translation: 'Stop! We are only asking whether you want tea or coffee').

See also **Humour, sense of**; **Meeting**

Effect, knock-on
= phrase: unintended consequence

Knowledge that is always retrospective. Like the much-quoted example of chaos theory in action – a butterfly flapping its wings on one side of the world causing a storm on the other side of the world – in the office one thing, indubitably, leads to another.

Usage** – Caught-out managers explaining why it has all gone wrong and why it cannot be their fault as it was impossible to foresee the unforeseen problem.

See also **Hindsight**

Ego, without
= phrase: ignoring one's own interests or feelings

This is the difficult, far-off goal of Zen Buddhism that emphasises the necessity of daily meditation and self-abnegation.

Usage* – In job adverts where *empathy* is highlighted as an important skill: 'You will be *without ego* while commanding high levels of credibility with colleagues' (translation: 'The martinet drop-to-the-floor-and-give-me-20-press-ups approach hasn't worked – low morale, high absenteeism, falling productivity – so we're going for the softly-softly-catchee-monkey approach to see what happens'). It should be noted that Zen Buddhism has few disciples in the looking-after-number-one bedlam of the office.

See also **Empathy**

80/20 rule
= n: Pareto's Law – named after Vilfredo Pareto, a 19th-century economist, this states that 80% of the sales or profits of an organisation come from 20% of its products/services/people

A *rule of thumb* that, once recognised, invites a series of swingeing judgements.

Usage**** – *Ambitious managers*, with typical chutzpah, cloaking their ignorance in pseudo-scientific analysis; *Thesaurus managers* who will always refer to it as Pareto's Law because they think it makes them appear more intellectual; and *Unironic managers* because they think it *is* a law.

See also **Ambitious manager**; **Rule of thumb**; **Thesaurus manager**; **Unironic manager**

Eleventh hour, at the
= phrase: a late intervention

The point at which a senior manager becomes involved in a piece of work.

Usage ** – Plaintive managers: 'Everything was sorted, then *at the eleventh hour* he has to go and stick his oar in . . .'

See also **Sanity check**

Empathy
= n: an ability to enter another's personality and imagine his experiences

The predisposition of an optimist.§

Usage *** – *Californian managers* habitually: it is the wellspring of their *enthusiasm*; also in job adverts for *Human Resources* roles – the irony here, of course, is that in the office this is precisely the quality that will be of least use.

See also **Californian manager**; **Ego, without**; **Enthusiasm**; **Human Resources manager**

§ It was Gore Vidal who wisely said: 'Whenever a friend succeeds, a little in me dies.'

Empower
= v: to authorise; to give power to

A promise that is rarely what it seems.

Usage ***** – A malignant expression that has spread like a

flesh-devouring virus. It is especially popular with cynical *HR managers*; as well as managers saying what is expected of them: 'What we are about is *personal growth*, self-development, new *opportunities*, in a word – *empowerment*' (translation: 'If you fail I will make sure you are booted out faster than you can say, "*Stephen R. Covey*"'). It is also beloved of *HR managers* who have read the work of *inspirational* business *gurus* and wish to indicate that they share a similarly radical view of how the company might be self-managing, where the old oppositional language of 'workers' and 'managers' is redundant; where everyone is *empowered* to make decisions appropriate to the task in hand. A good test of empowerment is to ask for a sabbatical or to park in a director's designated parking space.

See also **Stephen R. Covey**; **Growth, personal**; **Guru**; **Human Resources manager**; **Inspirational**; **Opportunity**

End to end
= phrase: unbroken; continuous

From a distance, many organisations look like one of Escher's[§] puzzles – impossible but apparently continuous.

Usage *** – *IT managers* talking extravagantly about their latest *plan*: 'It's an *end to end* organic user-friendly structure' (translation: 'It's a bit ramshackle but it's the best I could do in the circumstances given the lack of time, people, expertise and money').

See also **IT manager**; **Plan**

[§] M. C. Escher (1898–1972) was a Dutch graphic artist who is best known for creating optical illusions based on mathematical concepts.

Energy, high levels of
= phrase: showing great vigorousness

A state in which much can be achieved – for good and bad.

Usage *** – In job adverts for all kinds of positions: 'This is an

all-action role demanding *high levels of energy*' (translation:
'You will belong to us body and soul. Cancel all commitments.
In fact, cancel your life').

See also **Always-on**; **Full-on**; **24/7**

Enthusiasm
= n: strong interest; great eagerness

Contagious like laughter – or influenza. An affliction affecting
the young and inexperienced disproportionately. The only cure
is time.

Usage **** – In job adverts for all kinds of positions; blustering
managers covering their ignorance; *Ambitious managers*
who know that it is an essential term to demonstrate their
commitment and *passion*; *Californian* and *Hungry managers*
habitually; also cynical *HR managers* habitually.

See also **Absolutely!**; **Ambitious manager**; **Californian
manager**; **Commitment**; **Human Resources manager**;
Hungry manager; **Passion**

Entrepreneur
= n: a person undertaking a business for profit

An *enthusiast* whose God is Profit.

Usage * – Executives selling themselves to the media; job adverts
for senior positions: 'Energetic, *enthusiastic* and *entrepreneurial*, and able to identify *opportunity* and potential' / 'High-impact
executive who thrives in an *entrepreneurial* environment.
Results-focused and able to *inspire* others to over-deliver.
Self-motivated with the desire to *make a difference* and to
move the business towards a much better place' (translation:
'We have absolutely no idea what to do next – do you?')

See also **Difference, making a**; **Enthusiasm**; **Ground floor, get in
on the**; **Inspirational**; **Monster**; **Opportunity**; **Results-focused**

Envelope, pushing the

= phrase: finding new ways of working; going beyond current limits

A performance that often ends badly.

Usage ***** – A phrase from the world of aeronautics (and popularised via Tom Wolfe's *The Right Stuff*) that is an Offlish poeticism. It is used routinely by executives and senior managers to make any kind of new development, no matter how humble in reality, sound like a revolutionary – and danger-filled – leap forward: 'It's a new experience for everyone. A *greenfield opportunity*. We are really *pushing the envelope* here.' A substitute phrase is 'stretching the envelope'.

See also **Greenfield opportunity**

Excellence, centre of

= phrase: something demonstrating superior values

A short prayer.

Usage ***** – A fanciful expression of wish-fulfilment. At best it is a statement of sincerity rather than fact and is used to encourage either the speaker himself or his audience that some magical transubstantiation will occur to create something tangible, durable and profitable from their vaporous promises. Therefore, it is perfect for the half-truths contained in job adverts as well as the tub-thumping rah-rah of *Sales managers*.

See also **Sales manager**

Eyes and ears

= phrase: consciousness

The two most important of the five senses and a vital source of information about the world.

Usage ** – *Sales managers* (invariably to other sales personnel) who believe that because they occasionally speak to customers (but, in truth, no more than is strictly necessary) they are the only people who really know what is happening in the company: 'Don't forget. We are the lifeblood, the *eyes and ears* of this company.'

See also **Coal face, at the**; **Sales manager**; **Sharp end, at the**; **What's what**

Face time
= n: a meeting

A formal rendezvous. The ability to converse is one of the things that distinguish man from the animals.

Usage **** – Power-crazed executives and senior managers – 'I could really do with some *face time* on this' – to indicate that they have deigned to spend a portion of their precious working day with you in person as opposed to sending commands by BlackBerry, courier, email, fax, letter, messenger, mobile, skywriting and so on and so on.

See also **Meeting**

Fag packet, back of a
= phrase: an outline or sketch of a problem

Generally held to be the best place to make the necessary calculations to assess the financial viability of a project or piece of work.

Usage **** – Managers everywhere reflecting on the preparation undertaken to create the latest company *strategy*: 'Who are they trying to kid? This is just Mickey Mouse *back of a fag packet* kind of stuff'; also *No-nonsense managers* who haven't the patience to wait for, or intelligence to understand, a considered financial analysis.

See also **Bean counter**; **No-nonsense manager**; **Strategy**

Fast-track

= v: to accelerate

A shuffling of the pack.

Usage *** – A vogue word used for setting new priorities. It is used by harassed managers who suddenly realise that the project intended for, say, London is stuck in a siding several miles outside Nantwich: 'I want to clear the decks and *fast-track* this one.' It is also used by pompous *HR managers* of *high-flying* individuals who have been designated for rapid advancement up the corporate *ladder*.

See also **High-flier; Human Resources manager; Ladder**

Fat man in the canoe

= phrase: an influential person

An obvious obstruction. If he moves, then everyone else must move too . . .

Usage ** – Far-sighted managers anticipating a crisis; rueful managers who did not.

See also **Bigwig; Monster**

Feedback

= n: comments or reactions

Communication that tends to travel in one direction only.

Usage ***** – Originally a technical word from electronics and the biological sciences, this has achieved ubiquitous usage as a lazy synonym for 'comments' or 'responses'. It is now a kind of nervous tic signalling the end of a presentation or *meeting*. Except for the *Californian* and *Training manager*, all such information is, of course, routinely ignored. Is there a deadlier phrase in office life than: 'Now, could I ask for your *feedback*?'[§]

See also **Californian manager**; **Input**; **Meeting**;
Training manager

§ Dear reader, if you have any thoughts or opinions on *Ducks in a Row*
then please write to Short Books at 15 Highbury Terrace, London, N5
1UP or email info@shortbooks.biz

Feet, went in with both
= phrase: excessive vigour

An assault that, on the football field, would necessitate a straight
red card; in certain situations in the office, however, it may be
viewed with straightforward approbation.

Usage ** – Anyone, especially *Sales managers*, who believes that
forceful argument is more effective than reasoned and rational
debate: 'You should have seen him. We had hardly started when
he *went in with both feet*. Roy Keane or Robbie Savage would
have been proud.'

See also **Card, red**; **Passion**; **Sales manager**

Fences, mend
= phrase: restore good relations; issue an apology

An ancient art.

Usage ** – Members of the board constantly; the *Ambitious
manager* for self-advancement; the *No-nonsense manager* rudely;
the *Machiavellian manager* for his own long-term purposes.

See also **Ambitious manager**; **Machiavellian manager**;
No-nonsense manager

Finger on the pulse
= phrase: display knowledge or understanding

A skill best left to trained medical professionals.

Usage ** – Managers everywhere affecting an embarrassing

Finance manager

Quiet and determined, he is a dour grafter and a perfectionist. Often hidden away for long periods, he is nonetheless hugely influential. He is happiest when working alone with a calculator and a set of complicated spreadsheets – 'crawling all over the figures'. He is much maligned and much misunderstood by his colleagues who, for the most part, cannot follow his esoteric art. His view is uncomplicated: it is 'all about *the numbers*'. He has never learned the skills of the politician; a brusque truth-teller who makes everyone uncomfortable, he is reviled but also greatly feared, and should, if at all possible, be avoided.§

See also **Apples with apples**; **Bake**; **Ballpark**; **Bean counter**; **Chest, war**; **Cost-effective**; **Drill down**; **Fund, slush**; **GIGO**; **Guesstimate**; **Number crunching**; **Numbers, the**; **Robbing Peter to pay Paul**; **Stack up**

§ The collective noun for *Finance managers* is a sum.

---

streetwise argot, but especially *Sales managers*, of all ages, whose belief in the efficacy of '*street cred*' is unshakeable.

See also **Sales manager**; **Street cred**; **Word on the street**

Firing on all cylinders
= phrase: making every effort

A word of warning: the office can be a dangerous place.

Usage ** – *Sales managers* describing either themselves or, less frequently, their *team*.

See also **Gas, cooking with**; **Sales manager**; **Team**

Fish, mad as a
= phrase: an eccentric or unconventional person

An enthralling sight.

Usage** – Managers – originality being, more often than not, misunderstood – describing a (more successful) *colleague*. In the hurly-burly of the office it is useful to have a supply of 'mad as . . .' analogies.

See also **Bag of snakes, mad as a**; **Box of frogs, mad as a**; **Colleague**; **Python, mad as a writhing**; **Swing bin, mad as a**

FIFO
= acronym: Fit In Or F**k Off

In difficult times, sacrifices are sometimes required from the individual for the greater good.

Usage***** – Smiling *HR managers* explaining to the board the latest *downsizing* or '*people*' initiative; also *No-nonsense managers*.

See also **Downsize**; **Human Resources manager**; **No-nonsense manager**; **People**

Fix, quick
= n: a swift solution

Always prefixed by the negative.

Usage*** – Newly appointed executives who are in a hurry to establish a reputation for '*making it happen*'; and managers everywhere in a wide variety of situations as a catch-all, playing-for-time response to criticism or to a request for a speedy answer to a *problem*: 'Of course, there's no *quick fix*.'

See also **Fruit, low-hanging**; **Happen, make it**; **Problem**

Flagpole, run it up the
= phrase: get a response to an idea or proposal

An occasion that generally demands a formal response.

Usage ***** – *Unironic managers*, always cheerily: 'Why don't we bounce [or 'kick'] a few ideas around, *run them up the flagpole* and see if they get a salute?' For many *Unironic managers* it is their preferred, albeit elaborate, method for testing a commercial or managerial hypothesis.

See also **Unironic manager**

Flip side
= n: the alternative version

There are always two sides to any argument . . .

Usage *** – . . . unless you are dealing with a *CEO*; any director or senior manager; or a *Machiavellian, No-nonsense, Sales* or *Samurai manager*. It is a phrase used mostly by middle and junior managers who haven't yet realised that they have lost the argument. It is also a gift to the *Ambitious manager*, allowing him to present opposing views – 'the other side of the coin' – to see which one is the most popular.

See also **Ambitious manager**; **CEO**; **Machiavellian manager**; **No-nonsense manager**; **Sales manager**; **Samurai manager**; **Sword, double-edged**

Floor, back to the
= phrase: reacquaint oneself with the fundamentals

An opportunistic holiday from reality (such as Marie Antoinette and her tour of duty as a shepherdess) that allows an individual to return to his daily routine refreshed.

Usage *** – A recent Offlish invention via the popular reality-television programme that has rapidly established itself as an essential demonstration of good corporate leadership. The phrase is used by *CEOs* showing the popular touch for the PR department to exploit to the full: 'This isn't just lip service to improving communication. This is real *back to the floor* information-gathering from the ground up. Nothing is off-limits. There'll be free and frank discussions with everyone, at all levels.' Such occasions will, of course, be elaborately stage-managed so that the great man will learn nothing to overturn his hobby-horses and long-standing prejudices. Nor will he break sweat. The photograph in the trade press of his grinning face above a gleaming staff toilet will wholly disguise the fact that it was his PA who wore the rubber gloves and administered the bleach.

See also **CEO**

Floor, blood on the
= phrase: passionate argument

A metaphor.

Usage*** – Bruised and battered managers recounting an especially tempestuous *meeting*: 'It was ugly in there. Everyone at one another's throats. It was a real *blood on the floor* situation.' Debate and argument in the office can be fierce and uncompromising, but should this ever become more than a metaphor, you should consult urgently with a lawyer.

See also **Blamestorm**; **Meeting**

Flying by the seat of one's pants
= phrase: acting on instinct; unpremeditated

A popular magic trick.

Usage** – Beleaguered executives, as a private confession; harassed managers everywhere; *Lackadaisical managers* for whom it is one of their few principles. The influence of the Magic Circle in the office has been generally underestimated.

See also **Lackadaisical manager**

Food chain

= n: a hierarchy

An efficient system that is the result of thousands of years of evolutionary forces.

Usage *** – Anyone, except the *CEO*, lamenting their place in the corporate hierarchy: the *CEO* being the lion king of the corporate jungle dining on the board directors who feast on the senior managers who gobble up middle managers who eat the junior managers who feed on the staff who pick at the serfs.

See also **Clout**; **Order, pecking**

Football, fantasy

= n: an unrealistic scheme

A popular variation on the beautiful game.

Usage * – A phrase via *Premiership English* (probably created by *Ron Atkinson*) that is popular with *No-nonsense managers*: 'That'll never work; it's just *fantasy football*, that is.'

See also **Ron Atkinson**; **No-nonsense manager**; **Premiership English**

Forward, going

= phrase: in the future

An everyday blessing.

Usage ***** – A very important Offlish term: a verbal flourish that is used by everyone, everywhere to foretell a brighter tomorrow: '*Going forward* we will … [insert the relevant promise here].' Variations of the phrase are 'On a *going forward* basis' and 'on a *go forward* basis'.

Freak, control

= n: a person with an abnormal need to control events

A sick individual requiring immediate segregation, otherwise the consequences for others can be serious.

Usage *** – Jealous managers complaining about a (more successful) *colleague.*

See also **Colleague**; **Micromanager**

Fresh air, breath of
= phrase: new and refreshing

A tribute that soon becomes stale.

Usage ** – Managers welcoming the arrival of an executive who 'tells it like it is'. Shortly afterwards, the newcomer is inevitably seen for what they are – an insufferable egotist. It is also used by journalists of opinionated, straight-talking *CEOs* who make writing copy very easy with a string of heretical, headline-making opinions – until, that is, the first indication of a downturn in the company's performance or expectations.

See also **CEO**

Fromage, grand
= n: an influential person

A *player.*

Usage * – *Thesaurus managers.*

See also **Bigwig**; **Cheese, big**; **Player**; **Thesaurus manager**

Front, leading from the
= phrase: demonstrating leadership

An act of great courageousness.§

Usage ** – *PR managers* with a script; *Sales managers* as a channel for their belligerence; *Samurai managers* as a compulsion. For different reasons it is viewed with disapproval

by the *Californian manager* and the *Machiavellian manager.*
Tom Peters advocated a form of leadership he called MBWA
(Managing By Wandering Around), while for the *No-nonsense
manager* Sir Alex Ferguson/Arsène Wenger/José Mourinho/
Mick McCarthy is the example to follow (please delete
as applicable).

See also **Californian manager**; **Machiavellian manager**;
Tom Peters; **Premiership English**; **Public Relations manager**;
Sales manager; **Samurai manager**

§ It was St Matthew who wisely said: 'For many are called, but few
are chosen.'

Fruit, low-hanging
= n: the quickest and easiest solutions

A popular harvest (and a cause of great distress to Adam and Eve).

Usage ***** – *Unironic managers* to indicate the presence or
absence of simple answers: 'I didn't know where to start, there
was so much *low-hanging fruit*'/'I've trawled through these
reports but I just can't see any *low-hanging fruit.*' Whenever
you hear this phrase you have a choice. First, wherever you are,
pick up your things, go back to your desk, collect your most
important personal belongings and head for the exit. You may
wish to say a swift and smiling goodbye to your workmates. In
any event, like Lot escaping Sodom and Gomorrah, do not look
back. This is not the place for you. Alternatively, smile broadly
and knuckle down to the drudgery of corporate serfdom.

See also **Fix, quick**; **Unironic manager**; **Wins, quick**

Full monty
= n: everything included

An attitude of naked *enthusiasm* that is difficult to ignore.

Usage * – Derived perhaps from Sir Montague Burton, the

founder of the Burton's menswear stores, and supplier of a large proportion of the uniforms and demobbed suits in the second world war, or perhaps from General Montgomery's habit of wearing, in contradiction of the rules, the badges of both the army and the navy on his beret. It has been given wider currency via the antics of the male strippers in the successful British film *The Full Monty*. The phrase is often used by *No-nonsense managers* to create the impression that nothing of any importance has been omitted from a piece of work.

See also **All-singing-all-dancing**; **Enthusiasm**; **Kitchen sink**; **No-nonsense manager**

Full-on
= adj: committed; excessive

A stance that announces itself in an unmistakable manner.

Usage **** – A dark term that should trigger a Pavlovian response: an immediate and unrenounceable distrust of the user. Anyone prepared to use the phrase without an ironic inflection is almost certain to be a wide-eyed *workaholic* sociopath whose entire existence begins and ends with the office. Such individuals are dangerous and should, if at all possible, be avoided. They can only bring trouble; or worse, generate even more work for you. It is used by the *Hungry manager* who never turns off his BlackBerry: 'We are pretty *full-on* around here. We're *24/7*. Work hard. Play hard. That's our motto.'

See also **Always-on**; **CrackBerry**; **Hungry manager**; **24/7**; **Workaholic**

Fund, slush
= n: a cash reserve (originally from the money raised by selling a ship's *slush* or grease from the galley)

An essential principle of accounting.

Usage** – Canny *Finance managers* who have set aside monies to cover possible shortfalls in the budget. It may also be used by *Machiavellian managers* for greasing palms at opportune occasions.

See also **Finance manager**; **Machiavellian manager**

Future-facing
= adj: looking forward

A mongrel term: the offspring of fashion and balderdash.

Usage***** – Unblushing executives who don't care if they are talking nonsense; pretentious, jargon-ridden job adverts written by empty-headed *HR managers*; lazy managers who take refuge in Offlish rather than thinking for themselves; also *Unironic managers* who don't know any better.

See also **Human Resources manager**; **Unironic manager**

Game, name of the
= phrase: the plan of action

Admittedly in a different context, but this is a question asked by Abba some years ago.

Usage* – Baffled managers who 'just want to know what's going on. We're out of the loop on this one. What's *the name of the game* anyway?'

See also **Direction, strategic**; **Plan**; **Strategy**

GIGO
= acronym: Garbage In, Garbage Out

An unimpeachable formula.

Usage** – A term from computing (pronounced 'guy – go') used by *IT managers* as they try to rectify a programme or report; *Finance managers* with a shake of the head in despair at the idiotic gaffes made by their innumerate colleagues.

See also **Finance manager**; **IT manager**

Gas, cooking with
= phrase: achieving peak performance

A metaphor that should, in fact, only be used literally.

Usage **** – *Sales managers* excitably taking credit for sales figures; *Unironic managers* who believe it to be an accurate reflection of the facts: 'Wow! We're on a roll here. We're really *cooking with gas* on this one!'

See also **Firing on all cylinders**; **Sales manager**; **Unironic manager**

Geek
= n: a person who is socially awkward

An individual with specialist knowledge.

Usage *** – Managers everywhere of their introverted and tongue-tied IT *colleagues.*

See also **Anorak**; **IT manager**; **Nerd**

Global
= adj: worldwide

A very large area bigger than, for example, England.

Usage ** – Directors ignoring the facts; grandiloquent *management consultants* without regard to the facts; also *entrepreneurs* who regard facts as inconvenient. *Unironic managers* will inevitably tag on the tired catchphrase 'Think *global*; act local.'

See also **Entrepreneur**; **Management consultant**; **Unironic manager**

Go for it!

= phrase: not to stop until the goal is reached

A noisy slogan that is easier to say than to define.

Usage**** – Everyone from the company receptionist to the *CEO* who believes that it is a moral duty to be consistently cheerful and noisily positive in the workplace.

See also **CEO**; **JFDI!**

Go, let

= v: to make redundant

An unsolicited leave-taking and a melancholy phrase expressing in compact form the heartbreaking transience of life.

Usage** – Senior managers on the sad fate of a former *colleague*, usually uttered in a resigned, there-but-for-the-grace-of-God tone; also *No-nonsense managers* on the inevitable end of a former *colleague*, always in a brisk, well-he-had-it-coming accent.

See also **Colleague**; **Contribution**; **Downsize**; **No-nonsense manager**; **Reasons, personal**; **Restructure**

Goal, own

= n: a goal scored for the opposition; an action that backfires

Sometimes a tragedy, more often a farce.

Usage** – Managers everywhere of the latest corporate gaffe or a *colleague*'s blunder.

See also **Colleague**; **Shoot oneself in the foot**

Goal-driven

= adj: strongly motivated to achieve tasks

A mongrel term: the offspring of fashion and bunkum.

Usage***** – Unblushing executives who don't care if they are talking nonsense; pretentious, jargon-ridden job adverts written by empty-headed *HR managers*; eager-to-please candidates who hope that Offlish will make them appear in-the-club, businesslike, pliant and, therefore, suitable for corporate employment; on-the-make managers who use Offlish gobbledegook to show their seeming *commitment* to the cause; lazy managers who take refuge in Offlish rather than thinking for themselves; also *Unironic managers* who don't know any better. (Substitute phrases are 'goal-directed', 'goal-focused' and 'goal-oriented'.)

See also **Commitment**; **Human Resources manager**; **Unironic manager**

Goalposts, moving the
= phrase: setting new objectives

A tradition in the office that has not, as yet, been adopted by the Football Association.§

Usage *** – Managers everywhere complaining of their dithering superiors.

§ The occasion in 1977 at Wembley where Scottish fans tore down the goalposts after a victory over England has, mercifully, proved to be an isolated example.

Google
= n & v: the Google website; to use the Google website

An educational tool without parallel.

Usage *** – The panjandrum of search engines that, fast and simple to use, has transformed working life and produced a new demotic verb. Many working hours slip painlessly by on www.google.com. For information on news and current affairs, listings, sport, travel, hobbies, or just for following a trail of *stuff*, it is unsurpassed. For work itself, of course, it is virtually useless.

Granular

= adj: made up of small particles; a detailed analysis

A thorough approach that encompasses the minute, the infinitesimal and the teensy-weensy.

Usage **** – A synonym for 'detailed' used by pompous executives and managers in *meetings* and presentations: 'It necessitated a *granular* approach to *problem*-solving' (translation: 'We want you all to understand and acknowledge that we have worked very, very hard').

See also **Drill down**; **Meeting**; **Problem**

Gravitas

= n: a serious disposition

The father of pomposity and inaction.

Usage ** – In job adverts for all kinds of senior roles: 'A strong *motivator*, with an ability to pull as well as to push, you will have the energy and *gravitas* to succeed in a highly competitive sector'; also candidates in application letters for senior roles.

See also **Motivation**; **Vision**

Greenfield opportunity

= n: a new initiative

An environmental hazard.

Usage **** – A stupid phrase – like '*pushing the envelope*' or '*thinking outside the box*' – intended to hoodwink and distract. It is especially popular, therefore, with *management consultants*, as well as *PR managers* and executives; for example, when describing a new initiative where it is used as evidence of the company's *entrepreneurial* courageousness: 'A principal element of our *strategic vision going forward* is the utilisation of high-yield *greenfield opportunities*' (translation: 'Do I sound statesmanlike? A leader of men?').

See also **Box, thinking outside the**; **Entrepreneur**; **Envelope, pushing the**; **Forward, going**; **Management consultant**; **Public Relations manager**; **Strategy**; **Vision**

Green light
= n: a signal to proceed; permission to start

A necessary stage in any project.

Usage** – Managers who have difficulty distinguishing between the view of the car park from their office and the Hollywood hills: '*Guys*, the auditioning is over. I'm going to give you a *green light* on this one. We're good to go.' It is also sometimes used as a toe-curling verb: '*Team*, I'm going to *green light* this one.'

See also **Guys**; **Team**; **Tick in the box**

Groundbreaking
= adj: new; innovative

An idle boast.

Usage*** – In job adverts for senior positions where it is usually so much padding; callow candidates at interviews keenly repeating the key statements from the advertisement in order to demonstrate that, while they may have no understanding whatsoever of what the job entails, they can at least show that they have paid attention to the advert; also candidates exaggerating their achievements in their *CV*.

See also **CV**; **Hype**; **Ideas-driven**

Ground floor, get in on the
= phrase: to be involved from the beginning

Generally held to be the easiest way to enter a building.

Usage*** – Senior managers who want to make a mark and to get a reputation for *entrepreneurialism*: 'This is a gold-bottomed sure thing. We must *get in on the ground floor* if we don't want to get left behind. In terms of *opportunity*, this is big' (translation: 'I've got a bit of a hunch . . .').

See also **Entrepreneur**; **Opportunity**

Grown-up
= adj: characteristic of an adult

A stage in life where childish behaviour is a choice.

Usage *** – Exasperated managers in *meetings* asking 'just for once' whether they might enjoy 'a *grown-up* conversation' with a *colleague*.

See also **Colleague**; **Meeting**; **Throw one's toys out of the pram**

Growth, explosive
= phrase: a rapid increase

A spectacular event recorded in legend and ancient stories.

Usage *** – A Chairman addressing the shareholders – and hoping for a miracle; *Sales managers* addressing the board – and hoping for a miracle. For the *Marketing manager*, every marketing campaign is 'aggressive' and holds the promise of '*explosive growth*' – even those that lose lots of money.

See also **Marketing manager**; **Sales manager**

Growth, personal
= n: a person's development towards maturity

A principle promulgated by idealists, but most often by the wealthy and successful.

Usage ***** – Hand-wringing *Training managers* constantly; earnest *Californian managers* constantly; also cynical *HR managers* as often as they believe it is necessary to demonstrate their good faith.

See also **Alarm bells ringing, set**; **Californian manager**; **Empower**; **Human Resources manager**; **Training manager**

Guesstimate
= n: an estimate based on inadequate information

The starting point for a rigorously rational and detailed analysis.

Usage**** – Time-pressed managers; *Lackadaisical managers* habitually; *No-nonsense managers* who do not have the patience to bother with a financial analysis; also *Finance managers* committing professional hara-kiri: 'It's a bit of a *guesstimate* at the moment. Somewhere between 50 quid and a round million . . . Er, we haven't finished *crunching the numbers* yet.'

See also **Ballpark**; **Finance manager**; **Lackadaisical manager**; **No-nonsense manager**; **Number crunching**

Guru
= n: a spiritual teacher; a person who starts a movement (originally from Sanskrit)

A truth-maker who is adept at selling his wisdom.

Usage*** – Writers on business affairs who create any kind of abstract system to describe the world of business will eventually be lauded by the media as a '*guru*' (even if their ideas are foolish, long-winded, platitudinous or just plain bonkers). Self-styled *inspirational CEOs* who are always looking at the '*big picture*' are also lazily referred to by the media as '*gurus*'.

See also **Charlatan**; **Stephen R. Covey**; **Empower**; **Charles Handy**; **Inspirational**; **Tom Peters**; **Picture, big**

Guys
= n: a group of people (of either sex)

The correct collective term for addressing a *team*, a *meeting*, or any group of *people*.

Usage***** – Managers everywhere.

See also **Aligned**; **Cocks on the block**; **Huddle**; **Meeting**; **People**; **Team**

Hackneyed
= adj: made commonplace by overuse

Familiarity breeds contempt – and childish behaviour.

Usage** – Managers everywhere dismissing any idea or proposal from a *colleague*: 'It's a solid enough piece of work, but a wee bit *hackneyed*' (translation: 'Damn! Why didn't I think of that?')

See also **Colleague**

Handbags
= n: a skirmish

A battle which may be fierce, but which is lacking in dignity.

Usage* – Managers describing a disagreement using football terminology: 'To be fair, it wasn't hammer and tongs. There was a bit of a to-do, but it was just *handbags* really.'

See also **Premiership English**

Handbags, dancing round the
= phrase: useless prevarication

A tedious dance marathon where no prizes are awarded.

Usage**** – An economical means of signalling that the *meeting* should come to a conclusion: 'This is just consensual bollocks. Let's get on with this and stop *dancing round the handbags*, shall we?' The *No-nonsense manager*'s distrust of debate and discussion is profound and his belief in action unswerving.

See also **Houses, go round the**; **Meeting**; **No-nonsense manager**; **Shop, talking**; **Titanic, rearranging the deckchairs on the**

Handcuffs, golden
= n: sum of money; package of benefits

A traditional form of encouragement.

Usage *** – Contented executives who have been promised benefits over a period of time if they stay with the company; grumbling managers.

See also **Hello, golden**; **Sweetener**

Handshake, golden
= n: sum of money; package of benefits

A traditional show of gratitude.

Usage *** – Contented executives who have been promised a sum of money in compensation for the loss of a job (or early retirement); grumbling managers.

See also **Parachute, golden**; **Time-rich**

Hands-off
= adj: disengaged

The preferred management style of the executive who needs time and space to consider the *big picture*.

Usage ** – Unhappy and exhausted managers who necessarily have to get on with the *dirty work*.

See also **Picture, big**; **Work, dirty**

Hands-on
= adj: personally engaged

The preferred management style of the manager who believes wholeheartedly in the adage 'If you want a job doing well, it is better to do it yourself'.

Usage *** – Unhappy and frayed managers describing their

Micromanager boss; job adverts for sales positions; candidates at interviews ingratiating themselves.

See also **Micromanager**

Charles Handy

A wise and profound writer; the lay-preaching, portfolio-living *inspirational* creator of a series of books (such as *Age of Unreason*, *The Empty Raincoat* and *The Hungry Spirit*) in which every kind of business and life decision is described in terms of oh-so-easy-to-follow secular parables.

See also **Guru**; **Inspirational**

Alan Hansen

Cerebral former Liverpool and Scotland defender. Now a popular pundit on *Match of the Day* who is famous for his forthright and saturnine views. His most engaging locutions have consistently enriched *Premiership English* and Offlish by extension.

See also **Alarm bells ringing, set**; **Pear-shaped, go**; **Percentages, play the**; **Premiership English**; **Results**

Happen, make it
= phrase: to bring about a result

A much-used rallying cry or incantation.

Usage **** – Managers everywhere as the culmination of a *team* talk or presentation, either as an open threat or a covert petition:

'So, come on, let's close ranks and *make it happen, guys.*'

See also **Guys**; **Team**

Hat
= n: covering for the head; area of responsibility

An essential element to any business outfit which can be used for many other purposes, such as for talking through, throwing into the ring, keeping things under and, most commonly, pulling things out of.

Usage** – Managers everywhere either in exasperation or, more usually, as a point of pride. A variety of headgear is essential for the hard-pressed manager who will be called upon to change his apparel on a regular basis as the company's *strategy* swings hither and thither: 'In the morning I had my marketing *hat* on. In the afternoon my sales *hat*. Tomorrow it's logistics.'

See also **Strategy**

Hauled over the coals
= phrase: chastised

A terrible punishment routinely administered.

Usage* – Rueful out-of-favour managers.

See also **Hindsight**

Headbang
= n: a meeting to generate innovative ideas

A more physical version of a *brainstorm*.

Usage*** – *Brand managers* who have used '*brainstorm*' too many times before; also *No-nonsense managers* who believe that thinking is fundamentally wimpish.

See also **Brainstorm**; **Brand manager**; **No-nonsense manager**

Heads up

= n: a summary provided ahead of a fuller explanation;
a warning

In nature, alertness and survival are often intertwined.

Usage** – Managers whenever a short summary is given for
the benefit of *colleagues*: 'This is in the nature of a *heads up*,
guys.' Perhaps it originated from the recognition that in any
presentation or meeting the majority of your *colleagues* will
have their heads down because they are daydreaming or in a
state of denial that they are present at all.

See also **Colleague**; **Meeting**; **Warning, health**

Hearts and minds, winning

= phrase: gaining support

A form of blandishment that covers the spectrum from
substantial cash incentives to clandestine brainwashing.

Usage*** – Managers under pressure to achieve a result when
they know that the proposal, project or task is likely to be
received badly because it is ill-conceived, badly timed or
fundamentally foolish. It is popular with credulous *Californian
managers* and is also used often by the board and *PR managers*,
although rarely in public.

See also **Californian manager**; **Public Relations manager**

Heavyweight

= n: an exceptionally capable person

Possibly a *player*, certainly a *big hitter*.

Usage* – Chairmen searching for a leader to rescue the company;
job adverts for senior roles; directors with wary respect for a
business opponent; deferential managers.

See also **Cheese, big**; **Hitter, big**; **Player**

Hello, golden

=n: a sum of money or package of benefits

A traditional welcome.

Usage *** – Contented executives who have been promised a sum of money to join a company; grumbling managers.

See also **Handcuffs, golden**; **Sweetener**

Heroic

= adj: showing bravery or courage; befitting a hero

Behaviour that demands acclaim and long-lasting recognition.

Usage ** – Managers ironically celebrating a *colleague*'s misplaced efforts.

See also **Colleague**; **Muppet**

Hero-to-zero

= n: a formerly successful person

A common trajectory and a suitable subject for tragedy.

Usage ** – Senior managers on the sad fate of a former *colleague*, usually in a resigned, there-but-for-the-grace-of-God tone; *No-nonsense managers* on the sad fate of a former *colleague*, always in a brisk well-he-had-it-coming accent; also tabloid journalists of out-of-favour *CEOs*.

See also **CEO**; **Colleague**; **No-nonsense manager**

Hiccup

= n: a convulsive gasp; a hitch

A useful word that allows everyone to gain perspective on a catastrophe.

Usage ** – Desperate managers hoping to get a second chance; nervous senior managers explaining that every *strategy* needs time to deliver the expected *results*, and that progress should never be expected to be uniformly smooth: 'No, it's not a big *problem*. It's just a bit of a *hiccup*. A little blip. It just needs time to *bed in*' (translation: 'Please don't sack me. It won't happen again. I'll work night and day to keep it hidden from the board'). It is also used by *CEOs* in interviews with journalists irritably dismissing a massive setback: 'No, it's not a big *problem*. It's just a bit of a *hiccup*' (translation: 'Ask a better question').

See also **Bed in**; **Hindsight**; **Problem**; **Results**; **Ride, bumpy**; **Strategy**

High-flier[§]

= n: a person enjoying great success

And who therefore has so very far to fall . . .

Usage *** – Envious managers of their (more successful) *colleagues*; journalists patiently waiting for an executive to make a miscalculation.

See also **Colleague**

[§] Defined as 'One that carries his opinions to extravagance' by Samuel Johnson in his *Dictionary*.

High-profile

= adj: in the public eye

A position of prominence which guarantees that one's virtues – and faults – are highly visible.

Usage **** – In job adverts for senior positions and not-so-senior positions: 'A vanguard, *high-profile* [or 'pivotal'] role that will further propel you on an upwards career trajectory to establish wider *strategic* impact'; cynical *HR* interviewers who aren't averse to stretching the truth (translation: 'We call it *high-profile*; therefore, you get a lower salary').

See also **Human Resources manager**; **Strategy**

Hindsight

= n: wisdom after the event

A rare ability enjoyed by important and influential persons only.

Usage ** – *CEOs*, at the company conference, explaining how, when everything was in place to deliver the company's *strategy*, a wholly unforeseen occurrence (such as the fact that customers didn't want what the company was selling) derailed the plans. By contrast, any manager using a similar excuse would be likely to be lambasted for his stupidity and disorganisation.

See also **CEO**; **Hauled over the coals**; **Hiccup**; **Strategy**

Hit the ground running

= phrase: begin energetically and enthusiastically

A cause of many accidents.

Usage *** – Blustering managers and disciplinarians seeking to encourage their *teams*; also senior managers to new starters, often couched as an offer of support: 'We really need you to *hit the ground running* from day one and to set the pace' (translation: 'You belong to me now').

See also **Energy, high levels of**; **Team**

Hitter, big

= n: an exceptionally capable person

Possibly a *player*, certainly a *heavyweight*.

Usage ** – Chairmen on the sort of leader they need to rescue the company; job adverts for senior roles; directors with a wary respect for a business opponent; deferential managers.

See also **Cheese, big**; **Fromage, grand**; **Heavyweight**; **Player**

Hobson's choice

= n: no choice at all (after Thomas Hobson (d. 1631),[§] a carrier who hired out horses on the basis that customers had to take the horse nearest the door)

Such as *between the Devil and the deep blue sea* or *a rock and a hard place*.

Usage** – Harassed managers self-pityingly describing their lot; also stoical managers who have been given an impossible task. (The solution, which is well understood by *Ambitious managers*, is to delegate.)

See also **Ambitious manager**; **Barrel, over a**; **Catch-22**; **Devil and the deep blue sea, between the**; **Rock and a hard place, between a**

[§] A famous person in his day: John Milton even wrote two memorial poems about him.

Holistic

= adj: all round; examining the whole

A treatment that, sadly, often fails.

Usage *** – A vogue word whose derivation is via philosophy and medicine, and which is popular with the pretentious. In most contexts it means little more than looking at a problem from more than one viewpoint. *Ambitious managers* like its pseudo-intellectual, 'green' associations, but even more its difficult-to-define airiness: 'It's a *holistic* response to a complex *problem.*' For *Californian managers*, on the other hand, with its suggestion of organic healthfulness, it remains a defining principle: 'I want a *holistic team* approach. All-for-one-and-one-for-all.'

See also **Ambitious manager**; **Californian manager**; **Problem**; **Synergy**; **Team**

113

Home, working from

= phrase: salaried work undertaken away from the office

Time given over to necessary rest and private reflection.

Usage ** – Senior managers who are overtired, sick of the sight of their colleagues, or who haven't yet read all the Sunday papers.

See also **Sickie**

Honest, to be

= phrase: candid; straightforward

Mmmm . . .

Usage **** – Managers everywhere, prefacing a less than wholly truthful statement.

See also **Feedback**

Hoops, jump through the

= phrase: a pointless exercise

An athletic performance that rarely gains applause.

Usage *** – Drained managers. The influence of the circus in the office has long been underestimated.

See also **Balls in the air**; **Tick in the box**; **Whip, crack the**

Horns, take the bull by the

= phrase: assume control

A word of warning: the office can be a dangerous place.

Usage ** – The unchanging advice of the *No-nonsense manager*.

See also **No-nonsense manager**

Hot-desking
= v: a practice whereby work stations are not allocated to specific workers but are taken by the first person to arrive

A cold comfort.

Usage *** – A discipline that – outside IT companies – is still rare despite persistent advocates. Known as 'location independent working', it is hugely unpopular for obvious reasons and, tellingly, never extends to the rank of senior manager and beyond. Where it has been adopted, there has been, however, one unquestionable benefit: a massive reduction in the population of soft animal toys.

Houses, go round the
= phrase: to take a circuitous route

A familiar journey undertaken, despite warnings against monotony, on a regular basis.

Usage ** – *No-nonsense managers* in *meetings*: 'Let's kick this into touch once and for all and move forwards. We don't want to *go round the houses* again on this one.'

See also **Handbags, dancing round the**; **Knitting, stick to the**; **Meeting**; **No-nonsense manager**

Huddle
= n & v: a conference; to crowd together

A *meeting* where information is passed on, orders are given and punishments administered.

Usage ***** – *Californian managers* who believe that '*people* are our number-one asset': 'Let's have a quick *huddle* and chew the fat'; managers everywhere adopting a *touchy-feely* mode: 'Can we *huddle*, *guys*?'

See also **Californian manager**; **Hauled over the coals**; **Guys**; **Meeting**; **People**; **Powwow**; **Touchy-feely**

Human Resources manager

Formerly known as the Personnel manager, or in some self-styled 'progressive' companies as the *People* manager, he is responsible for payroll, pensions, recruitment and, perhaps most importantly, morale. Dedicated and reserved, he is the backbone of the company. On behalf of the workforce he is a devoted form-filler and form-creator as well as a good-humoured tyrant for the correct procedures (look out for his informative or *inspirational* posters). He believes in '*teams*', '*partnerships*', a '*no blame culture*' and a large, comfortably appointed office for his many cabinets of personnel files. He has the onerous task of having to pass judgement on his fallible colleagues. His watchwords are '*skill sets*', 'competencies' and 'proficiencies'. Such is his stature and unimpeachable reputation that he is often involved on those occasions, unavoidable even in the most successful companies, where there is, regrettably, '*bad news*' to impart (his knowledge of the law relating to the termination of contracts is formidable). His intellectual reach and fastidiousness is perhaps best demonstrated in his distinctive prose style (as seen in his lovingly crafted job adverts). He is distrusted by everyone and he should, if at all possible, be avoided.[§]

See also **Action-oriented**; **Appropriate**; **Asset**; **Autonomy**; **Axe**; **Buzz**; **Culture, no blame**; **Empathy**; **Enthusiasm**; **Fast-track**; **FIFO**; **Growth, personal**; **High-profile**; **Influencer**; **Input**; **Inspirational**; **Interpersonal**; **Meritocracy**; **Mile, go the extra**; **Motivation**; **News, bad**; **Objective**; **Own**; **Partnership**; **People**; **Skill set**; **Square peg in a round hole**; **Strategy**; **Succession planning**; **Surprises, policy of no**; **Swim, sink or**; **Team**; **Team, catalyst**; **Thinking, blue-sky**; **Track record**; **Wood, dead**; **Workshop**

[§] The collective noun for *Human Resources managers* is a cadre.

Humour, a sense of

= phrase: ability to make or take a joke

A ticklish question: one man's guffaw being another's tumbleweed.

Usage ***** – In job adverts for all kinds of positions: 'You will have a seasoned *sense of humour*' (translation: '. . . we're *mad* here, we are'); candidates confirming same in application letters. *Ambitious managers* laugh at the same punchlines as senior managers; *IT managers* laugh at their own jokes exclusively; *No-nonsense managers* have an earthy *sense of humour* that extends from *Carry On double entendres* to actress-said-to-the-bishop jokes; *Sales managers* like practical jokes (the swift removal of a chair causing a painful fall, for example); *Thesaurus managers* enjoy puns; *Unironic managers*, meanwhile, only use sanctioned office humour.

See also **Ambitious manager**; **Cigar, close but no**; **Doh!**; **Easy tiger!**; **Hungry manager**; **IT manager**; **Let's not go there**; **No-nonsense manager**; **Pigs, flying**; **Pressure!, no**; **Sales manager**; **Thesaurus manager**; **Unironic manager**; **Z**

Hungry manager

His work is his life. He has many strong beliefs about targets and deadlines and, more generally, '*making it happen*'. His watchwords are '*commitment*' and '*passion*'; he is, in his own words, '*full-on*'. He is a *workaholic* who is perpetually tense and anxious; he has no *sense of humour* and is a hard taskmaster who arrives in the office early and leaves late. He is, therefore, easy to distinguish from an affable, genial conversationalist. He is detested by everyone and should, if at all possible, be avoided.

See also **Always-on**; **Ante**; **Commitment**; **CrackBerry**; **Enthusiasm**; **Full-on**; **Happen, make it**; **Humour, sense of**; **Passion**; **24/7**; **Up for it?**; **Workaholic**

Hymn sheet, singing from the same
= phrase: collective action and responsibility

All together now . . .

Usage ***** – *Unironic managers* monotonously. Should this become something more than merely metaphorical, it may be time to redraft one's *CV*.

See also **CV**; **Ducks in a row**; **Unironic manager**; **Wavelength, on the same**

Hype
= n & v: excessive or extravagant language; to promote

A simple language to learn that is growing in popularity and is very useful in many circumstances.

Usage **** – An important and thriving branch of Offlish whose advance appears unstoppable. It is used by executives as well as by almost all kinds of managers, but especially excitable *Marketing managers* whose relationship to reality is tangential at best. *No-nonsense managers*, it should be noted, are not native speakers and struggle with the vocabulary: 'I tell you it was nothing but waffle. *Hype* and nothing else.'

See also **Groundbreaking**; **Marketing manager**; **Mega**; **World-class**

Ideas-driven
= adj: innovative

A mongrel term: the offspring of fashion and pretension.

Usage *** – Managers who describe themselves as 'creative'; *Marketing managers* as a nebulous peacock-proud self-description; sardonic *management consultants*; unblushing executives who don't care if they are talking nonsense; pretentious, jargon-ridden job adverts written by empty-headed *HR managers*; eager-to-please candidates who hope that Offlish will make them appear in-the-club, businesslike, pliant and, therefore, suitable for corporate employment; on-the-make managers who use Offlish gobbledegook to show their seeming *commitment* to the cause; lazy managers who take refuge in Offlish rather than thinking for themselves; also *Unironic managers* who don't know any better.

See also **Commitment**; **Groundbreaking**; **Human Resources manager**; **Management consultant**; **Marketing manager**; **Off-the-wall**; **Unironic manager**

Impact
= n & v: a strong effect or influence; to have a strong effect

A moral touchstone.

Usage ***** – Everyone, as an unlovely noun: '*The numbers* had an *impact* on everyone in the room.' It is also one of the most important Offlish verbs, as it shows forcefulness and *enthusiasm* which are both prime virtues in the office: 'How are we *impacting* on *the numbers* with this one?' Standard English equivalents are the less dramatic 'affect' or 'alter'. But '*impact*' itself has been judged too weak and has spawned both '*impactful*' and '*impactfulness*': 'We're looking for an *impactful* promotion'/'The *impactfulness* of the promotion will be crucial.'

See also **Enthusiasm**; **Numbers, the**

Improvement, continuous
= n: unceasing progress

Shangri-La.

Usage ***** – Company bulletins; managers everywhere from the highest to the most junior; also raring-to-go candidates and babbling job adverts for senior positions: 'You will be a *future-facing strategic* thinker with an exceptional *track record* of delivering results through setting *inspirational* standards and *driving proactive continuous improvement.*'

See also **Drive**; **Future-facing**; **Inspirational**; **Proactive**;
Strategy; **Track record**

Influencer
= n: a person who has an effect on another

Capable of many guises, from a bringer of balm to a brazen
bludgeoner.

Usage *** – *Californian* and *Training managers* habitually; in
job adverts for senior positions: 'Personally confident,
collaborative, with exceptional communication and negotiation
skills – an *influencer* with commercial savvy' (translation: 'No
one talks to each other here. It's a daily battleground. A war of
attrition. You will need the magnetism of a Mandela or a Gandhi
in order to make headway'). Also jaded *HR managers* in
interviews: 'Are you an *influencer*?' (translation: 'Are you *up for*
sacking people?').

See also **Californian manager**; **Human Resources manager**;
Training manager; **Up for it?**

Input
= n & v: views, comments, recommendations; to contribute
information

A request that, unfortunately, is rarely ignored.

Usage **** – Cynical *HR managers* who couldn't care tuppence
for anyone's opinions: 'Your *input* would be warmly welcomed';
managers who know they have to be seen to be asking the
question but have no intention of doing anything with the
answers: 'Sorry, I drifted off for a moment. What were you saying?';
also *Californian managers* habitually and hopefully: 'I'd really
value your *input* and *feedback*.'

See also **Californian manager**; **Feedback**; **Human Resources
manager**; **Talk**

Inspirational

= adj: bringing inspiration

The breath of life; the highest calling.

Usage ***** – Managers everywhere, but especially cynical *HR managers*, who don't believe a word of it, and *Californian managers*, for whom it is their consuming aim and desire. It is also used by self-aggrandising executives and managers to describe themselves. When you hear this word you have a choice. First, wherever you are, pick up your things, go back to your desk, collect your most important personal belongings and head for the exit. You may wish to say a swift and smiling goodbye to your workmates. In any event, like Lot escaping Sodom and Gomorrah, do not look back. This is not the place for you. Alternatively, accept the proffered advice and then knuckle down to a long life of corporate serfdom.

See also **Ron Atkinson**; **Box, thinking outside the**; **Californian manager**; **Cat, fat**; **Charlatan**; **CEO**; **Stephen R. Covey**; **Guru**; **Mentor**; **Monster**; **Wow factor**

Interface

= n & v: a boundary; to interact

A coming-together that runs the gamut from misunderstandings and friction to argument and confrontation.

Usage ***** – An ugly Offlish term that is becoming increasingly common in standard English. It is widely used by cynical *HR managers*, earnest *Californian managers* and, of course, *Unironic managers*. *IT managers*, on the other hand, use it in a technical sense only. It can sometimes be used as an absurd verb: 'Let's *interface* next week over lunch, yeah?'

See also **Californian manager**; **Human Resources manager**; **IT manager**; **Unironic manager**

Interpersonal

= adj: occurring between people

A coming-together that is rarely reciprocal.

Usage ***** – Another ugly Offlish term that is becoming increasingly common in standard English. It is widely used by cynical *HR managers*, earnest *Californian managers* and in job adverts for a variety of positions: 'strong *interpersonal* skills are a prerequisite' (where it means approximately 'talking to people').

See also **Californian manager**; **Human Resources manager**

IT manager

Shy and introverted, he is a technical genius whose role is incomprehensible to others. He is, therefore, generally unappreciated by his workmates. He is a specialist and his vocabulary, which is continually mutating as technology evolves, is hermetic and understood only by his fellow IT workers.§ He is mocked by everyone and he should, unless his expertise is required, be avoided.§§

See also **All-singing-all-dancing**; **Anorak**; **Bandwidth**; **Critical path**; **End to end**; **GIGO**; **Geek**; **Humour, sense of**; **Interface**; **Nerd**; **User, end**; **World-class**

§ His recurrent terminology would include, for example, 'ADSL', 'application', 'architecture', 'Bluetooth', 'bps', 'broadband', 'cookies', 'firewalls', 'HTML', 'IP', 'ISDN', 'LANs', 'PAN', 'PDA', 'POTS' ('plain old telephone system' – a rare IT joke), 'scalability', 'server', 'SQL', '3G', 'URL', 'WAN', 'WiFi' and so on and so on. Elsewhere in the office this is known as 'double Dutch', 'techie-speak' or, according to the *No-nonsense manager*, 'bollocks'.

§§ The collective noun for *IT managers* is a programme.

Jerry-built
= adj: something made without regard for quality

A man-made structure.

Usage* – Managers damning anything from a *colleague*'s report to the company's *strategic* five-year plan.

See also **Colleague**; **Strategy**

Jigsaw, the final piece of the
= phrase: the last piece in a puzzle

The completion of a puzzle that can be enjoyed again and again.

Usage**** – The fanfare announcement that the *CEO* has completed the corporate jigsaw and has created the '*dream team*' is often overthrown within months by the need to re-jig the board due to evidence of hilarious incompetence, someone leaving 'to further their career elsewhere'/'spend time with their family'/ 'for *personal reasons*' or because of a *restructure* demanded by the parent company or macroeconomic changes – or just because the easily-bored *CEO* fancies 'a bit of a shake-up'.

See also **CEO**; **Musical chairs**; **Reasons, personal**; **Restructure**; **Team, dream**

Jobsworth
= n: a person who works strictly within his allotted role

An individual with strong opinions and views about workplace proprieties.

Usage** – Thwarted managers.

Journeyman
= n: a reliable but not outstanding worker

A wise man who knows well his limitations.

Usage** – *No-nonsense managers* definitively dismissing a *colleague*.

See also **Colleague**; **No-nonsense manager**; **Premiership English**

JFDI!
= acronym: Just F*****g Do It!

A brash statement intended to banish confusion.

Usage***** – The transformation of Nike's vacuous Just Do It! shoutline into a blunt managerial instruction is often accompanied by a ghastly and complicit 'we-are-all-in-this-together' rictus. It is used by managers for whom heavy-handed irony is a principal means of communication, as well as by managers for whom heavy-handed irony is a way of papering over the unpalatable truth that the *JFDI!* principle is the foundation of corporate relationships: 'I hear you. But this isn't a debate. It's a *JFDI!* situation.'[§]

See also **Cocks on the block**; **Go for it!**

[§] Consider wearing a sports-style self-printed T-shirt under your suit with the emblazoned legend Just Say No. Even the smallest gesture of abandon and defiance can be hugely satisfying.

KISS
= acronym: Keep It Simple Stupid

A kiss should always be rewarded with a kiss. In this case, a Glasgow kiss.

Usage*** – *Sales managers*; also *Unironic managers* for whom it has the authority of on-high wisdom.

See also **Knitting, stick to the**; **Sales manager**; **Unironic manager**

Keep on an even keel
= phrase: in a stable condition

A skilled hand is always required on the tiller, especially with the threat of stormy weather.

Usage *** – *Worldly-wise managers* dispensing unasked-for advice; executives affecting an insufferable folksy tone.

See also **Ride, bumpy**; **Worldy-wise manager**

Keep one's powder dry
= phrase: show caution; circumspection

Useful advice – if one has a musket.

Usage ** – *Worldly-wise managers* passing on hard-won wisdom to young managers: 'I'd advise you to wait and see; *keep your powder dry*; and only pull the trigger when you see the whites of the goalie's eyes.'

See also **Worldly-wise manager**

Key
= n & adj: the essential; the most important

A *key* word in the office.

Usage ***** – Everyone, everywhere, constantly.

See also **Core**

KPIs
= acronym: Key Performance Indicators – a set of statistics regularly reported that are used to measure the performance of a business or area of a business

A jumble of facts in search of a narrator.[§]

Usage ***** – Baffled managers everywhere; it is an obsession of the *Finance manager* and a blessing for the under-seige executive who, with a bit of judicious *tweaking*, can always find something positive from the weekly deluge of statistics; also *Ambitious managers* who recognise that the careful use of acronyms creates a sound impression of professionalism.

See also **Ambitious manager**; **Finance manager**; **Tweak**

§ It was Benjamin Disraeli who supposedly said: 'There are three kinds of lies: lies, damned lies and statistics.' (A quotation attributed to him by Mark Twain in his *Autobiography*.)

Kitchen sink
= n: a basin; the entirety

An important facility in the office.

Usage *** – This is the Offlish equivalent of the proverb 'Leave no stone unturned'. It is often used as a general encouragement: 'Let's throw the *kitchen sink* at this, *guys*'; but also retrospectively by fatalistic managers to explain that, although something went wrong, nothing else could have been done: 'We gave it everything. We threw the *kitchen sink* at it, we did.'

See also **Full monty**; **Guys**

Knitting, stick to the
= phrase: to avoid complication

A practical pastime mostly favoured by the elderly that is periodically re-presented by the media as a fashionable art.

Usage ***** – Executives urging a return to traditional strengths: 'We should respect our heritage and *stick to the knitting*'; *No-nonsense managers* using this obscure Offlish term (probably invented by *Tom Peters*) to urge the *meeting* to return to the point under discussion: 'Stop poncing about. Let's get back *to the knitting*.'

See also **Basics, back to**; **Handbags, dancing round the**; **No-nonsense manager**; **Meeting**; **Tom Peters**

Knockout blow

= n: a winning punch; an elimination

A cartoon victory.

Usage** – Desperate *CEOs* exhorting the board to come up with an idea to destroy a rival. The influence of the noble art of boxing in the office has been generally underestimated.
A KO may be administered as a result of a rigorous training regime and a display of courage and ringcraft; alternatively, by a low-blow, eye-gouging, well-timed rabbit punch behind the referee's back or the gift of a well-stuffed brown envelope to the promoter.

See also **CEO**; **Ropes, on the**

Lackadaisical manager

A reliable presence in the office – when he can be located. On those infrequent occasions when he is sighted, he is always exceptionally affable and friendly. He is a fine conversationalist and storyteller who can, and does, talk to anyone. He has strong beliefs centred on individualism and freedom of expression. An independent person, he can on occasions be resistant to the usual rules of management and other standard workplace disciplines. He would describe his attitude to work as 'relaxed', and while his approach is an *inspiration* to some, to others it is a substantial vexation. There is, however, no need to avoid him, as he will take great trouble to avoid you.§

See also **Ballpark**; **Flying by the seat of one's pants**; **Guesstimate**; **Inspirational**; **Mañana**; **Overview**; **Problem**; **Rome wasn't built in a day**; **Rule of thumb**

§ The collective noun for *Lackadaisical managers* is a hammock.

Ladder

= n: a structure used for climbing

A useful item, but take care: a momentary lapse of concentration has caused many a painful fall.

Usage *** – Cynical *Human Resource* directors implying that advancement is simple, open to all and inevitable; in job adverts written by empty-headed *HR managers* promising rapid corporate advancement; also disillusioned or desperate managers in moments of private gloom: 'What's wrong? Why can't I climb up the *ladder*?'

See also **Human Resources manager**; **Team player**

Lamb, sacrificial

= n: a young sheep used as a sacrifice

An animal with an important role in the office.

Usage *** – Bewildered managers who have been offered up by their boss; relieved managers who have seen peers offered up by their boss.

See also **Scapegoat**

Land

= v: to make happen; to secure

A dangerous manoeuvre that has resulted in many accidents.

Usage ***** – An Offlish commonplace used in *meetings* – instead of the standard English 'do' – by managers and executives everywhere to underline their vigorous determination. It is also a favourite of jargon-spewing *management consultants* as well as *Ambitious managers* (faking interest as usual) and *Unironic managers*, who are all Offlish devotees: 'Who is going to *land* this?'/'We need to *land* this baby PDQ?' '*Action*', '*drive*', '*nail*' and '*own*' have similar meanings and are widely used as substitutes.

See also **Action**; **Ambitious manager**; **Drive**; **Land**; **Management consultant**; **Meeting**; **Nail**; **Own**; **Unironic manager**

Leading-edge
= adj: in the forefront

A promise that is often not delivered.

Usage **** – In job adverts for positions describing the company's profile: 'We are a *leading-edge* [or 'breaking-edge' or 'cutting-edge' or 'industry-leading'] company/organisation' (translation: 'We are on a par with some of our competitors'); desperate candidates repeating the advert: 'I'm really keen to work for a *leading-edge* company. It's exactly what I'm looking for at this point in my career' (translation: *For God's sake* give me a job! I've been out of work for six months and I'm over my head in credit card debt').

See also **Blue chip**

Learnings
= n: useful knowledge acquired through study

Knowledge that, if used correctly, can prevent the time-consuming process of *reinventing the wheel*.

Usage ***** – An Offlish word not found in standard dictionaries that is, nonetheless, in widespread usage, especially by *Californian* and *Training managers*: 'Vis-à-vis the project. What are the *learnings* here?'

See also **Californian manager**; **Dive, deep**; **Training manager**; **Wheel, reinvent the**

Left hand not knowing what the right hand is doing
= phrase: a confusing situation (via St Matthew 6:3)

The opposite of a sleight of hand. This can be amusing to

watch so long as you are not directly involved.

Usage*** – *Worldly-wise managers*; self-righteous managers who know that if *they* were in charge none of these problems would be happening: 'It was a complete *disconnect*. A right *shambles*. A case of *the right hand not knowing what the left hand was doing.*'

See also **Disconnect**; **Shambles**; **Worldly-wise manager**

Legs
= n: longevity

Always a question.

Usage** – *Sales managers* rapping the table: 'Let's get down to *brass tacks* here. Has it got *legs*?'

See also **Sales manager**; **Tacks, brass**

Let's not go there
= phrase: avoid the subject

Wise words.

Usage**** – Humourless senior managers in *meetings*, simultaneously as a means of keeping to the *agenda* and as a sanctioned example of corporate humour.

See also **Agenda**; **Humour, sense of**; **Meeting**; **Unironic manager**

Liar
= n: a person who lies, especially habitually

An individual with a different view of events to oneself.

Usage* – Managers everywhere of (more successful) *colleagues*.

See also **Colleague**; **Sales manager**[§]

[§] See Appendix One – Humour, a sense of: Examples

Life Coach

An experienced *mentor* who will listen to *problems* and offer dispassionate advice and suggestions to overcome professional dilemmas and difficulties.[§]

See also **Mentor**; **Problem**

[§] Online and telephone services are available as well as the premier face-to-face service. A fee list is available on application.

Line, dotted

= n: a printed line formed by dots where a signature should be added

....

Usage **** – Managers everywhere. It is also used to describe a managerial relationship whereby an employee does not have direct responsibility to a particular manager (hence the '*dotted line*'). This system is guaranteed to cause confusion and frustration, and is introduced by senior managers who are too lazy or stupid to find an effective solution. 'This is a marketing role with a *dotted line* into . . . um . . . um. Finance. No. HR. No. Sales. Is that clear?'

See also **Game, name of the**

Line in the sand, draw a

= phrase: an end point

A simple action, although rarely effective – as King Canute was, perhaps, the first to discover.[§]

Usage *** – A phrase, almost always used self-deludingly, to indicate that an agreement or new stage has been reached in a *meeting*.

See also **Meeting**

§ Historians are divided as to whether King Canute really believed he could stop the waves or was demonstrating to his court that he did *not* have divine powers.

Lips, read my
= phrase: an invitation to pay attention (popularised by George Bush Snr)

An invitation that should be declined.

Usage ***** – *No-nonsense managers* assuming a presidential haughtiness. One response guaranteed to get a reaction is to stare fixedly at your colleague's mouth for the rest of the conversation or *meeting*.

See also **Meeting**; **No-nonsense manager**; **Space, watch this**

Lion's mouth, put one's head in the
= phrase: endanger oneself

A death-defying act.

Usage *** – Any *Worldly-wise manager* 'worth his salt' will certainly advise against this perilous activity. The influence of the circus in the office has long been underestimated.

See also **Hoops, jump through the**; **Worldly-wise manager**

Long haul, in for the
= phrase: long-term view

An admirable stance . . .

Usage *** – . . . but one requiring moral rectitude and courage as well as abundant effort and resilience (translation:'. . . or until circumstances change'). It is used by Chairmen explaining to the City that the company's *strategy* will, eventually, produce 'real *results*', but that it will be 'tough' in the meantime; as well as by keen new recruits eager to say the right thing to impress their new boss: 'Oh yes, I'm *in for the long haul* all right' (translation: '. . . or until I get a better offer').

See also **Results**; **Strategy**

Lose / lose
= adj: an unfavourable outcome for both sides

A disappointing situation that, due to the very high levels of testosterone displayed in the majority of negotiations, is far more common than *win/win*.

Usage *** – Jaded experienced managers who know that there is nothing to be done; *Californian managers* in a sweat of anxiety.

See also **Californian manager**; **Win/win**

Loser
= n: a person who fails regularly

In the office there is a place for everyone.

Usage ** – Managers adopting a passé teenage argot to describe a *colleague* who is useless, clueless or far more successful than themselves.

See also **Colleague**; **Sucker**

Losses, cut
= phrase: forfeit in order to prevent a worse situation

The stroke of a utilitarian. Every successful General knows that to lose the battle is not necessarily to lose the war.

Usage * – Executives *pragmatically* accepting that there will have to be a '*restructure*' and a period of 'retrenchment' in order to satisfy the shareholders that the board's *strategy* is not at fault (and that their salaries and share options and health schemes are safe for the moment).

See also **Downsize**; **Pragmatic**; **Restructure**; **Strategy**

Lunch, power

= n: a business *meeting* over a meal

Depending on one's status in the *food chain*: a vastly expensive four courses in a top-class restaurant with a bottle or two of fine wine recommended by the sommelier; the set menu in the local trattoria; pasta and all-purpose tomato sauce in the canteen; an uninspiring sandwich on a park bench; four pints of Guinness, two packets of cheese and onion, a bag of salted peanuts and two pickled eggs.

Usage*** – Executives and *Unironic managers* without irony; everyone else with irony.

See also **Food chain**; **Meeting**; **Unironic manager**

Machiavellian manager

A *conspirator*, a figure in the shadows and a master of the orchestrated vendetta. He is a cunning, unprincipled politician, lacking morality. Wily and conscienceless, he is cold-blooded and exceptionally patient. An intriguer and a string-puller, the *Machiavellian manager*'s goal is corporate advancement, and his method (he is very skilled with a knife) is to leave a trail of the unattributable dead and the mortally injured. He is feared by all and he should, if at all possible, be avoided.§

See also **Agenda, hidden**; **Backstabber**; **Black arts**; **Boat, in the same**; **Cannon, loose**; **Conspiracy**; **Doomsday scenario**; **Flip side**; **Off-line**; **Smoke and mirrors**; **Snake in the grass**; **Titanic, rearranging the deckchairs on the**

§ The collective noun for *Machiavellian managers* is a cloak.

Mad Hatter's tea party
= phrase: an unruly occasion

Every office has its own set of rules that may, on reflection, appear somewhat eccentric.

Usage ** – Managers discussing an unproductive *meeting*: 'It was all over the place. A right *Mad Hatter's tea party*.'

See also **Meeting**

Management Consultant

Cocksure and colourful, he is a showman and a show-off. An egotist whose watchword is 'I', he provides beautifully packaged reports that elegantly state the obvious or respond to questions that were never asked about businesses of which he has no experience or understanding. He is always expensively coiffed and suited; his manner confident and energetic; his fees breathtaking. Nicknamed 'Hatchet' or 'Chainsaw', he is often 'parachuted' into a business for a specific task. He is a tremendous generator of jargon, a celebrated user and a talented originator of Offlish.§ It is a paradox that while his is a role to which many aspire, he is loathed by everyone. He should, if at all possible, be avoided.§§

See also **Action**; **Community**; **Drive**; **Global**; **Greenfield opportunity**; **Ideas-driven**; **Land**; **Nail**; **Objective**; **Paradigm shift**; **Partnership**; **Problem**; **Quality-driven**; **Sacred cow**; **Unthinkable, thinking the**; **Value-added**; **Vision**; **Workshop**

§ See Appendix Two – The Jargon of the Management Consultant

§§ The collective noun for *management consultants* is a bill.

Mañana

= adv: tomorrow; at some time in the future (Spanish for 'tomorrow')

A philosophical position deserving of respect.

Usage* – *Lackadaisical managers* for whom it is a principle, and long-serving managers who are certain that their job is safe (as it would be too expensive to make them redundant).

See also **Lackadaisical manager**; **Rome wasn't built in a day**

Marketing manager

A flamboyant and brave spirit who is the creative force of the business. He is an innovator who believes not in '*ticking the box*' but in '*thinking outside*' it (hence the casual corduroy rather than the formal suit). As he is '*ideas-driven*', it would be unfair to expect him to keep conventional hours or to follow standard procedures.§ His controversial approach is often misunderstood by his colleagues, but he is thick-skinned and used to brickbats.§§ He is often thoughtful and modest (although many of his colleagues would say that he has plenty to be modest about). His principal concerns are VFM (value for money), PVM (perceived value for money), OTS (opportunities to see) and *valued-added* ploys. His watchwords are '*opportunity*' and '*competitive advantage*'. He is a fervent advocate of the new over the old and is responsible for major commercial developments such as B2B (formerly known as the more staid business-to-business selling), B2C (business-to-customer selling), B2D (business-to-distributor selling), CRM (customer relationship marketing) and D2C (direct to consumer), as well as guerrilla and viral marketing (respectively, expensive eye-catching stunts and chain letters via email). These new disciplines have led to new vocabularies as well as longer job titles, larger offices and an array of perks. He is despised by everyone and should, if at all possible, be avoided.§§§

See also **All-singing-all-dancing**; **Aspirational**; **Box, thinking outside the**; **Competitive advantage**; **Consumer agenda**; **Customer-facing**; **Growth, explosive**; **Humour, sense of**; **Hype**; **Ideas-driven**; **Market-led**; **Mega**; **Opportunity**; **Paradigm shift**; **Results**; **Square, thinking outside the**; **Thinking, lateral**; **Tick in the box**; **Tongues, speaking in**; **USP**; **User, end**; **Value-added**; **Wash its face**; **Whistles, bells and**; **World-class**

§ See Appendix One – Humour, a sense of: Examples

§§ It was Bill Hicks who described those who worked in marketing as 'satan's spawn'. His straightforward advice was that they should 'kill themselves'.

§§§ The collective noun for *Marketing managers* is a fancy.

Market-led
= adj: following the needs of consumers

A mongrel term: the offspring of fashion and drivel.

Usage ***** – *Marketing managers* habitually; unblushing executives who don't care if they are talking nonsense; pretentious, jargon-ridden job adverts written by empty-headed *HR managers*; eager-to-please candidates who hope that Offlish will make them appear in-the-club, businesslike, pliant and, therefore, suitable for corporate employment; on-the-make managers who use Offlish gobbledegook to show their seeming *commitment* to the cause; lazy managers who take refuge in Offlish rather than thinking for themselves; also *Unironic managers* who don't know any better.

See also **Commitment**; **Human Resources manager**; **Marketing manager**; **Unironic manager**

Maverick

= n: a nonconformist (from Samuel Maverick, a 19th-century Texas cattle-raiser)

An idiosyncratic rule-breaker and *entrepreneur* whose gambles have been marvellously rewarded.

Usage*** – Fawning journalists; cowed executives and managers.

See also **Entrepreneur**; **Monster**

Meeting

= n: an assembly of people; a discussion

A coming-together to underline differences.

Usage* – Everyone, everywhere: *meetings* being the most effective means of filling the working day.§

See also **Blamestorm**; **Challenge**; **Correct!**; **Easy tiger!**; **Face time**; **Floor, blood on the**; **Grown-up**; **Guys**; **Handbags**; **Handbags, dancing around the**; **Heads up**; **Houses, go round the**; **Huddle**; **Interface**; **Mad Hatter's tea party**; **Line in the sand, draw a**; **Lips, read my**; **Lunch, power**; **No**; **Off-line**; **Park it (but leave the motor running)**; **Ps and Qs**; **Powwow**; **Respect, with all due**; **Shop, talking**; **SUMO**; **Sit down**; **Stall, set out one's**; **Take that on board**; **Talk**; **Talk until blue in the face**; **Throw the baby out with the bath water, don't**; **Thumbs-down**; **Time, at this moment in**; **War zone**; **When you're in a hole stop digging**; **Yes**

§ A memorable *New Yorker* cartoon has a businessman in his office on the telephone with the caption: 'Is *never* good for you?'

Mega

= adj: large; important; excellent

A flexible mathematical value as well as a general term of commendation.

Usage **** – A word that first emerged in the playground, it is used by managers and executives who wish to demonstrate their *commitment* or *enthusiasm*: 'This is a *mega opportunity*.' It is also an essential item of vocabulary for '*ideas-driven*' *Marketing managers* who communicate most effectively via the language of *hype*.

See also **Commitment**; **Enthusiasm**; **Hype**; **Ideas-driven**; **Marketing manager**; **Opportunity**

Mentor
= n: teacher

A guide. All *inspirational* leaders have had an experienced *mentor* to help them on their path to enlightenment. Today, this is the job of the *life coach*.

Usage ** – Earnest *Californian managers* offering their experience for the benefit of others; also image-conscious executives of a former *colleague* 'who was like a father to me and told me everything I know about the business'.

See also **Ron Atkinson**; **Buddy**; **Californian manager**; **Colleague**; **Inspirational**; **Life coach**

Mercurial
= adj: lively; changeable; likely to do the unexpected (from Mercury, the Roman god of merchandise, theft and eloquence; the messenger of the gods)

The progenitor of great things – and terrible blunders.

Usage * – A favourite of football commentators to describe titchy wingers with dazzling head-down dribbling skills such as Jimmy Johnstone, Charlie Cooke, Pat Nevin and Shaun Wright-Phillips (all capable of 'moments of magic', but just as likely to be a 'liability'). It is used by the media to describe a *CEO* who has ceased to be *inspirational* but is not yet sufficiently incompetent to be a *lame duck*.

See also **CEO**; **Duck, lame**; **Inspirational**; **Premiership English**

Meritocracy
= n: government by individuals selected according to merit

A utopian form of governance that has never resulted in a tangible success.

Usage** – Corporate literature; cynical *HR* managers: 'We believe in the virtuous circle of *meritocracy*' (translation: 'Keep your nose clean and your ear to the ground, do your time and we'll see what happens').

See also **Human Resources manager**; **Order, pecking**; **Succession planning**

Micromanager

He is a meticulous crosser of Ts and a dotter of Is. No detail is too small for his attention. Every piece of work is an occasion for epic fiddling, nitpicking and useless questioning. He is detested by all and he should, if at all possible, be avoided.§

See also **Freak, control**; **Hands-on**; **Problem**; **Results**; **Speed, up to**; **Ts and Cs**

§ The collective noun for *Micromanagers* is a pinpoint.

Midas touch
= n: the ability to turn a situation to one's financial advantage (from the Greek legend where Dionysus gave Midas the gift of making everything he touched – including food and drink – turn to gold)

A gift that swiftly becomes a curse.

Usage* - Jealous managers of a (more successful) *colleague*; journalists lauding a *CEO* whose *strategy* has brought about a 'textbook turnaround' or rapid improvement in the company profits. Once celebrated, they may legitimately begin to sharpen their pens for the inevitable falling-off.

See also **CEO**; **Colleague**; **Duck, lame**; **Hero-to-zero**; **High-flier**; **Strategy**

Mile, go the extra
= phrase: strenuous and special exertion

A word of warning: the office can be exhausting.

Usage** - All managers, but especially *Sales managers*, exhorting their *team* to even greater efforts: 'We have to be seen to be setting the pace, *guys*. I need you to pull out all *the stops*, throw the *kitchen sink* at it and *go the extra mile* on this one.'

See also **Guys**; **Kitchen sink**; **Sales manager**; **Stops, the**; **Team**

Mission statement
= n: a document that is a distillation of a company's purpose

The meeting-point between commerce and philosophy.

Usage***** - Executives and *Brand managers* habitually. *Mission statements* only exist in the corporate world.§ Ostensibly, companies use them to refine their commercial purpose so that this is clear both internally and externally, but this has now spilled over into a general urge to define and explain which has resulted in widespread nonsense and absurdity. *Brand* agencies have made mountains of cash in recent years advising anxious companies and institutions, large and small, about the usefulness of new *mission* (or 'positioning') *statements*. Hence British Rail once famously boasted that it was 'Getting there'.

See also **Brand**; **Brand manager**; **Difference, making a**; **Guru**; **Passion**; **Tom Peters**; **Vision**

§ Although this is not the view of recent business *gurus*, such as *Tom Peters*, and a large number of self-help titles that advocate self-branding.

Monday to Friday
= phrase: the working week

An exceptionally long period of time – approximately six or, sometimes, seven days in duration.

Usage *** – Formerly a reasonably accurate description of the working week, it is used by lazy journalists who still believe it to be true and by exhausted managers everywhere, with a world-weary ironic expression.

See also **Time-poor**

Monster
= n: a grotesque, cruel or wicked person

A charismatic individual with a hidden deformity.

Usage ** – Exhausted and belittled managers speaking in code of their boss: 'He's larger than life. An *inspiration*. A real force of nature. And he certainly gets things done' (translation: 'He is an egotistical, pig-headed, short-tempered, insanely demanding bully who is incapable of listening to another point of view').

See also **Act**; **Entrepreneur**; **Inspirational**; **Maverick**

Motivation
= n: an incentive

A stimulant with strong side-effects.

Usage **** – Executives monotonously, as they all believe their *motivational* abilities are exceptional; *HR managers* because it is in their job description; self-confident managers who live by the declension: 'I *motivate*/You manage/They dictate'; also *Californian managers* who believe it is a kind of sacred (although strictly non-denominational) duty to *inspire* their *team*.

See also **Californian manager**; **Human Resources manager**; **Inspirational**; **Team**; **Troops, the**

Multitask

= v: to undertake more than one piece of work simultaneously

A modern skill best demonstrated by working mothers and idle teenagers.

Usage** – Harassed managers, especially men who like to-do-one-thing-at-a-time; also over-committed Chairmen who have the onerous responsibility of having their PA juggle their diaries to accommodate a plethora of corporate junkets, business lunches and lucrative non-executive directorships.

See also **Balls in the air**

Muppet

= n: a foolish person; a victim

In the office there is a place for everyone.

Usage* – Gloating managers enjoying a *colleague*'s error of judgement or mistake: 'I ask you. What a *muppet*!'

See also **Colleague**; **Space cadet**

Musical chairs

= n: a party game for young children

In the office a game played by adults with very high stakes.

Usage*** – Disillusioned managers who did not get the position they were expecting; journalists mocking the latest executive comings-and-goings; also baffled managers who are in the dark: 'From where I'm sitting it just looks like *musical chairs*.'

See also **Can, left holding the**; **Jigsaw, final piece of the**; **Succession planning**

Nail
= v: to fix in place; to pin down; secure

Physical labour that, in order to avoid damage to clothing, is a task best undertaken with one's *sleeves rolled up*.

Usage ***** – An Offlish commonplace used in *meetings* – instead of the standard English 'do' – by managers and executives everywhere to underline their vigorous determination. It is also a favourite of jargon-spewing *management consultants* as well as *Ambitious managers* (faking interest as usual) and *Unironic managers*, who are all Offlish devotees: 'We need to *nail* this baby, *ASAP*. Let's *go for it!' 'Action*','*drive*','*land*' and '*own*' have similar meanings and are widely used as substitutes.

See also **Action**; **Ambitious manager**; **ASAP**; **Drive**; **Go for it!**; **Land**; **Management consultant**; **Meeting**; **Own**; **Unironic manager**

Navvy, working like a
= phrase: exceptionally industrious (from the Irish labourers who were famous for their ability to work hard)

A state of self-pity brought about by a period of sustained heroic achievement that has gone unrecognised and unrewarded.

Usage * – Managers, with a what-can-I-do grimace: 'I'd really love to help but I'm already *working like a navvy* at the moment' (translation: 'I'd rather stick pins in my eyes'). It is useful in the office to have a supply of 'working like a . . .' analogies.

See also **Dog, working like a**; **Stakhanovite, working like a**; **Trojan, working like a**

Nerd

= n: a foolish or weak person

An individual with specialist knowledge.

Usage *** – Managers everywhere, especially of tongue-tied or introverted IT *colleagues* who are widely seen as problem-makers as well as problem-solvers.

See also **Anorak**; **Colleague**; **Geek**; **IT manager**

Networker

= n: a person who talks regularly to other people in his profession or trade

A shallow conversationalist and serial seducer.

Usage **** – Managers of (more successful) *colleagues* who are more outgoing and sociable than themselves: in the office the adage 'It's not *what* you know but *who* you know' will never go out of fashion. It is also popular in job adverts for executive positions: 'An outstanding *networker* with excellent communication and negotiation skills'.

See also **Colleague**

News, bad

= n: negative information about recent events

Information that should only be divulged once every hiding place has been thoroughly investigated.

Usage **** – Terrified managers; executives looking for a patsy.

See also **Accelerator, take one's foot off the**; **News, good**

News, good

= n: positive information about recent events

Information that should be broadcast as soon as possible to as many people as possible.

Usage **** – Savvy managers who recognise that it is a tradeable commodity as it is far more important than mere *results*; also endangered managers – from the humblest beginner to the mightiest Chairman – desperate for a fact, statistic or story to deflect attention away from a major *problem*.

See also **KPIs**; **News, bad**; **Problem**; **Results**; **Upside**

Niche, carve out a
= phrase: create a comfortable position

A laborious task (although the larger the company, the smaller the effort required).

Usage * – Envious managers of a well-placed *colleague*: 'He's got his pipe and his slippers. Yes, indeedy, he's *carved out a* nice little *niche* for himself.'

See also **Colleague**

Nightmare
= n: a horrifying experience

For some unfortunates, an affliction that continues beyond childhood into adult life.

Usage *** – For *Dramatic managers* an all-too-common cry caused, for example, by a slightly longer than normal journey into work, receiving a request for a meeting with less than a fortnight's notice, the barista in Costa failing to offer a dusting of chocolate on a cappuccino, and so on and so on.

See also **Bombshell**; **Dramatic manager**

9 to 5
= phrase: the working day

An exceptionally long period of time – approximately nine or 10 hours in duration, although sometimes longer.

Usage*** – Formerly a reasonably accurate description of the working day; now merely the sandwich between commuting, early and late *meetings* and preparation for *meetings*, catching up with emails and telephone messages.

See also **Meeting**; **Play, end of**; **Time-poor**

No
= adv & n: a refusal or disagreement

Rarely the correct answer.

Usage* – Managers who wish that they could turn back the clock.

See also **Yes**

No such thing as a free lunch
= phrase: everything comes at a cost

A dictum that is true only part of the time.

Usage*** – An all-too-typical interjection from the *Worldly-wise manager*; however, executives may take a different view.

See also **Lunch, power**; **Worldly-wise manager**

No-brainer
= n: obvious; insignificant

A statement that can often reflect badly on the user.

Usage***** – All managers everywhere, but especially *No-nonsense managers* who dislike any kind of extended discussion:'This isn't *rocket science*. It's a *no-brainer*.' The *No-nonsense manager* is certainly correct to point out that there are many things in the office that are not worth thinking about.

See also **No-nonsense manager**; **Rocket science**

No-nonsense manager

Part barrow-boy, part bar-room brawler, he has a deserved reputation for bluntness. He is gutter-mouthed, does not regard good manners as useful in the workplace and likes to go '*tits out*' at every opportunity. He is notably illiberal in his political opinions: for him, *Guardian* readers are 'pinko sandal-wearing, muesli-eating whingers' and *Telegraph* readers 'limp-wristed, chinless, Barbour-wearing, Tory toffs'; and he is made uncomfortable by women in positions of authority. He will use *Premiership English* in most situations, as well as popular catchphrases and a baffling personalised rhyming slang (Britney Spears, T.Rex, Thomas the Tank, Hampton Wick, stick of rock, and so on and so on). He enjoys humour of a broad and carnivalesque nature (sex, breaking wind and *double entendres* feature prominently) and is likely to wear comedy cufflinks.[§] Usually he can be heard coming from afar and, therefore, he should be easy to avoid.[§§]

See also **Ballbreaker**; **Ballpark**; **Balls**; **Basics, back to**; **Bombshell**; **Bust, shit or**; **Cocks on the block**; **Cold, catch a**; **Dickswinging**; **Dog's bollocks, the**; **Fag packet, back of a**; **FIFO**; **Flip side**; **Full monty**; **Guesstimate**; **Handbags, dancing around the**; **Headbang**; **Hero-to-Zero**; **Horns, take the bull by the**; **Houses, go round the**; **Knitting, stick to the**; **Lips, watch my**; **No-brainer**; **Omelette, you have to crack eggs to make an**; **Premiership English**; **Rocket science**; **Rule of thumb**; **Shop, talking**; **Swim, sink or**; **Tin, does what it says on the**; **Titanic, rearranging the deckchairs**; **Tits out**

[§] Popular sets are: Love/Machine, On/Off, They think it's all over/It is now, Well/Hung.

[§§] The collective noun for *No-nonsense managers* is a heckle.

Non-core

= adj: not central; unessential

Yesterday's news.

Usage* – *CEOs*, when announcing a period of 'consolidation' following poor results: 'We are urgently reviewing our portfolio in order to come to a better understanding of our *core* and *non-core* competencies. We have learned a hard lesson, and *going forward* we need to pull the right levers, de-risk the operation, find our feet, manage expectations, come out fighting and get *back to basics*. The market has spoken and we are listening' (translation: 'It's a fiasco'). Privately, he will be demanding of the board a '*quick* and dirty *fix*'.

See also **Basics, back to**; **Bread and butter**; **CEO**; **Core**; **Downsize**; **Fix, quick**; **Forward, going**; **Key**; **Losses, cut**; **News, bad**; **Principles, first**; **Strategy**

0-60

= phrase: nought to sixty (miles per hour); exceeding expectations

A tactic popular with joyriders.

Usage**** – A phrase via motoring vocabulary (is there, perhaps, an academic somewhere toiling in a library to describe the impact of *Top Gear* on the evolution of the English language?) to describe a product that has sold faster than the budgeted figures. It is used by *Sales managers* who want to enthuse over a successful launch (and who, of course, are obsessed by the quality of their company car): 'It was a *0-60* situation and no messing' (translation: 'It's a miracle – everything just seemed to go to *plan*').

See also **Plan**; **Sales manager**

Number crunching

= n: the processing of numerical data

For many, a mouthful of gall and wormwood.

Usage *** – Contented *Finance managers*; bamboozled managers explaining a delay on a piece of work: 'Everything is in place ... er ... we're just *crunching the numbers*.'

See also **Bean counter**; **Finance manager**; **Guesstimate**

Numbers, the

= n: an arithmetical value; financial performance

An esoteric art for a few; for the rest a profound mystery.

Usage ***** – *Finance managers* in *meetings* – followed by a long and unfathomable disquisition;§ innumerate managers (a large constituency) in bafflement or awe; senior managers and directors pretending they know more than they do.

See also **Bean counter**; **Finance manager**; **Meeting**; **Results**; **Stack up**; **Wash its face**

§ Numbers, the fourth book of the Old Testament, describes the wanderings of Moses and the Israelites in the desert. The Hebrew title means 'in the wilderness'.

Objective

= n: the goal to which a person or set of persons is directed

A tedious and tiring business. In the office there is no *objective* other than the next *objective*.

Usage **** – *Objectives* only exist in corporate life or for a handful of extremists such as crazily determined would-be pop stars and insanely focused athletes. The word is used primarily by *HR managers* in connection with appraisals or performance reviews. '*Objective*' is also used routinely by managers everywhere foolishly or pompously as a synonym for 'what we [or, more usually, *you*] have to do': 'Your *objective* is to fill in this very, very long form very, very carefully/stay out of my goddamn way until next week/humour me by laughing heartily at my jokes (even the one I have told you umpteen times about the farmer, the sheep that is actually a dog and the *management consultant*)' and so on and so on.

See also **Human Resources manager**; **Management consultant**

Off-brand

= adj: a view that is not the stated company policy

A position adopted only by the foolish, the naive or the *maverick*.

Usage**** – Executives and *Brand managers* discrediting a *colleague* in the most forceful terms available to them: 'You're *off-brand*, my friend' (translation: 'What is it about the *brand* values that you don't understand? You doofus. You numpty. You simpleton'). (A popular variation is 'off-message'.)

See also **Brand manager**; **Colleague**; **Maverick**

Off-line

= adj: outside the meeting

Let's take this *off-line* …

Usage***** – *Machiavellian managers* who know they will be able to get what they want outside the *meeting*; managers who see that they are about to be publicly exposed and want to forestall uncomfortable questions while simultaneously appearing authoritative and knowledgeable: 'Let's not get bogged down on this one; we'll discuss it *off-line* and move on' (translation: 'Phew!'); also *Unironic managers* for whom this is the correct procedure.

See also **Machiavellian manager**; **Meeting**; **Park it (but leave the motor running)**; **Unironic manager**

Off-the-wall

= adj: unconventional

Imagination: a gift enjoyed by the few.

Usage ** – Managers who routinely describe themselves as 'creative'.

See also **Bag of snakes, mad as a**; **Box of frogs, mad as a**; **Fish, mad as a**; **Python, mad as a writhing**; **Swing bin, mad as a**; **Thinking, lateral**

Oh!

= interj: an expression of surprise

The sound of revelation.

Usage *** – Guilty managers who have been rumbled.

See also **Ah!**

Omelette, you have to crack eggs to make an[§]

= proverb: 'Said by way of a warning to someone who is trying to "get something for nothing"' (*Brewer's Dictionary of Phrase and Fable*)

Any chef will confirm this indisputable culinary fact.

Usage ** – For the *No-nonsense manager* this is an important concept with many useful applications.

See also **No-nonsense manager**; **Pragmatic**

[§] Originating from France in the mid-19th century, this proverbial saying has also been associated with noted *pragmatists* such as Robespierre, Napoleon and Lenin.

On-brand

= adj: in agreement with the stated company policy

A position adopted by the careful, the invisible and the loyal.

Usage** – Executives and *Brand managers* as a warning.

See also **Brand manager**

Opportunity
= n: a chance; an opening

A magical password; an 'open sesame' to a world of achievements and riches.

Usage**** – Down-on-their-luck managers hoping for better things; *Marketing managers* borrowing from the lexicon of *hype* once again. It is also popular in job adverts for all kinds of positions: 'The role is exciting and *challenging* – a major *opportunity* for someone with energy and *enthusiasm* who can grasp the nettle and *hit the ground running*' (translation: 'This is the third time we have advertised this position'). Candidates invariably 'relish' such '*opportunities*'.

See also **Challenge**; **Enthusiasm**; **Hit the ground running**; **Hype**; **Marketing manager**

Order, bang out of
= phrase: unconscionable

A terrible cry of anguish that can be heard from one end of the office to the other.

Usage** – Any manager who has been 'stitched up': 'That's BANG OUT OF ORDER, that is!'

Order of the boot
= phrase: made redundant

Justice dispensed with vigour.

Usage** – *No-nonsense managers* reflecting on a *colleague*'s sudden departure: 'One minute he was top dog and the next the head honchos decide he's persona non grata and he gets the *order of the boot*.'

See also **Colleague**; **No-nonsense manager**; **Things, bigger and better**

Order, pecking
= n: a hierarchy

A universal system of classification.

Usage **** – Managers everywhere, usually ruefully.

See also **Correct!**; **Food chain**; **Meritocracy**

Out, up or
= phrase: a system of preferment where individuals are either promoted or forced to leave

A competitive principle that Charles Darwin would have understood.

Usage **** – *Management consultants* and *Ambitious managers* approvingly; all other managers nervously jostling for position while looking back at the field.

See also **Ambitious manager**; **Card, red**; **Management consultant**

Outcome-driven
= adj: determined

A mongrel term; the offspring of fashion and gibberish.

Usage ***** – Unblushing executives who don't care if they are talking nonsense; pretentious, jargon-ridden job adverts[§] written by empty-headed *HR managers*; eager-to-please candidates who hope that Offlish will make them appear in-the-club, business-like, pliant and, therefore, suitable for corporate employment; on-the-make managers who use Offlish gobbledegook to show their seeming *commitment* to the cause; lazy managers who take refuge in Offlish rather than thinking for themselves; also *Unironic managers* who don't know any better.

See also **Commitment**; **Human Resources manager**; **Unironic manager**

§ The kind that ask shameless questions such as 'Can you improve on the best?' or 'Have you got what it takes?'

Overview
= n: a sketch or outline

A picture, it is said, is worth a thousand words.

Usage *** – Overworked managers, as it is all they have time for; *Lackadaisical managers*, as anything else is too much effort. *Thesaurus managers*, by contrast, prefer to deliver a *tour d'horizon*.

See also **Lackadaisical manager**; **Plate, enough on one's**; **Thesaurus manager**; **Tour d'horizon**

Own
= v: to assume responsibility

An act likely to result in the assumption of a considerable burden, comparable to a mortgage or other large debt.

Usage ***** – The *CEO* urging the board to accept responsibility: 'I need you to *own* this one' (translation:'. . . so if it bombs, I won't get the blame'); directors to their senior managers (translation:'. . . so if it tanks, I won't get the blame'); senior managers to their subordinates (translation:'. . . so if it goes belly-up, I won't get the blame'). Also cynical *HR managers* as well as earnest *Californian* and *Training managers* for whom *ownership* is an essential dogma. '*Action*', '*drive*', '*land*' and '*nail*' have similar meanings and are widely used as substitutes.

See also **Action**; **Californian manager**; **CEO**; **Drive**; **Human Resources manager**; **Land**; **Nail**; **Order, pecking**; **Training manager**

P45

= n: a tax form detailing one's previous employment

The sword of Damocles§ in the office.

Usage** – Frightened managers.

See also **Box, thinking outside the**

§ The legend is that (in the fourth century BC) Dionysius of Syracuse, wearying of Damocles's flattery, sat him under a sword hanging from a single hair.

Ps and Qs

= phrase: to be careful; to behave properly

A phrase whose origin is a mystery and which is somewhat difficult to define, yet is exactly right for certain delicate situations.

Usage** – Circumspect managers to their subordinates before they attend an important *meeting*.

See also **Ambassador**; **Meeting**

Parachute, golden

= n: sum of money; package of benefits

A traditional show of gratitude.

Usage*** – Contented executives who have been promised benefits if they have to leave a company; grumbling managers.

See also **Handshake, golden**

Paradigm shift

= n: an overturning of beliefs

A revolution by which the status quo is preserved.

Usage**** – *Management consultants* seeking to justify their grotesque fees: 'It's a leap of faith but our recommendations offer a *paradigm shift* for the organisation' (translation: 'Goodbye ...'); *Marketing managers* who are presenting a new piece of work and have used '*step change*' or '*sea change*' a hundred times before.

See also **Change, sea**; **Change, step**; **Management consultant**; **Marketing manager**

Park it (but leave the motor running)
= phrase: set aside an issue or question

A quick getaway from a *meeting* is often required.

Usage **** – *Unironic managers* chairing a *meeting*: 'We aren't progressing this. We need 100% *buy in* and at this juncture we aren't bringing everyone with us. Why don't we *park it – but leave the motor running*?'

See also **Buy in**; **Meeting**; **Off-line**; **Unironic manager**

Partnership
= n: joint activity; acting together

A relationship of reciprocal exploitation

Usage ** – Cynical *HR managers* who know that this is the kind of language they are expected to use and that it will also make them appear affable and straightforward; *Californian managers* for whom it is an unchallengeable credo; also *Unironic managers* for whom it is nothing more than the truth. *Management consultants*, meanwhile, with their customary majesterial disregard for the English language, refer to 'mutual *partnerships*' or even 'collaborative *partnerships*'.

See also **Californian manager**; **Human Resources manager**; **Management consultant**; **Unironic manager**

Party, working
= n: a group of persons assembled to report on a specific project

A contradiction.

Usage**** - Senior managers and executives who have recently attended a management training course.

See also **Team**

Passion
= n: enthusiasm

A fervid proclamation that should be delivered with great frequency, ideally, accompanied by loud voices and the beating of breasts.

Usage***** - In *mission statements*; executives speaking of the company's employees to the press; managers speaking of their *teams*; nervous candidates saying what they think is the right thing. It is also common in job adverts for all kinds of low-paid positions.

See also **Commitment**; **Enthusiasm**; **Feet, went in with both**; **Hungry manager**; **Mission statement**; **Tom Peters**

Pear-shaped, go
= phrase: awry

A silhouette that is often a cause of distress.

Usage*** - An obscure phrase that is popular with managers everywhere to describe all manner of mishaps. It is also common in *Premiership English*.

See also **Ron Atkinson**; **Alan Hansen**; **Premiership English**; **Tits up**

People

= n: a set of persons; a body held together by common beliefs or culture; a workforce

A collection of individuals.

Usage ***** – Beloved of HR departments, this is often used in empty phrases such as 'It's a *people* thing' or '*People* are our greatest *asset*'. (This last doctrine is unambiguously true until there is a *change* in circumstances whereupon the corporate mantra swiftly becomes '*the bottom line*'.)

See also **Asset**; **Bottom line, the**; **Change**; **Difference, making a**; **Downsize**; **FIFO**; **Guys**; **Restructure**; **Talent, pool of**; **User, end**; **Wood, dead**

PLU

= acronym: People Like Us

A doctrine that is generally regarded as antiquated.

Usage *** – Old-fashioned executives who wish to employ the 'right sort' and for whom avoiding contact with riff-raff (in other words, graduates from universities other than Oxbridge) is a priority.

See also **Boys, jobs for the**

Percentages, play the

= phrase: display prudence

A time-honoured tactic for the *risk-averse*.

Usage *** – Cautious managers, habitually; *No-nonsense managers* aping their hero *Alan Hansen*, for whom this is the unchanging foundation of footballing success.

See also **Alan Hansen**; **No-nonsense manager**; **Premiership English**

Tom Peters

Inspirational business *guru*, writer and speaker who identified the *'wow factor'* as critical to business success and whose philosophy might best be summarised by his apothegm: 'If it ain't broke, break it.' He came to prominence with *In Search of Excellence*, which was a worldwide bestseller. One of his less well known titles is *Brand You 50: Fifty Ways to Transform Yourself from an 'Employee' into a Brand that Shouts Distinction, Commitment and Passion.*

See also **Brand**; **Commitment**; **Guru**; **Inspirational**; **Passion**; **Wow factor**

Picture, big
= n: wide perspective

A popular genre for those with grandiose aspirations.

Usage ***** – An Offlish term in widespread usage: Chairmen announcing a new initiative to the City or shareholders: 'We've taken a step back and looked at the *big picture*' (translation: 'It's a rush job. We'll fill in the details later'); the board to senior managers: 'We've taken a helicopter view from 10,000 feet. It's *big picture* stuff' (translation: 'Now can you fill in the many gaps to make this work?'); everyone else (except the *Unironic manager*) incredulously. It is also used regularly by the *Ambitious manager* to make himself appear thoughtful and intelligent.

See also **Ambitious manager**; **Guru**; **Hands-off**; **Strategy**; **Unironic manager**

Pigeonhole

= v: to compartmentalise

A crude but serviceable classification system.

Usage*** – Sullen managers who believe that they deserve better.

See also **Order, pecking**

Pigs, flying

= phrase: an unlikely event

A common event.

Usage* – A popular jest with executives who have no *sense of humour*.

See also **Humour, sense of**

Ping

= v: to send an email or to alert someone to something

!

Usage** – An onomatopoeic word – formerly a technical term used to describe a submarine's sonar which became a term for a computer test communication – it is now widely used in the sense of 'send' or 'notify', often in the sense of 'dispose of'. 'Can you *ping* that on to Marketing?'

See also **Problem**

Pipedream

= n: a fantasy or unattainable hope

Originally experienced under the influence of opium.

Usage* – A manager's private assessment of the company's latest madcap, make-it-up-as-you-go-along initiative – or a *colleague*'s hilarious career *plans*.

See also **Colleague**; **Downshift**; **Plan**

Plan

= n & v: a design or scheme; to create a design or scheme

A godlike vision of the future created by mortal men and women.

Usage*** – Everyone, everywhere, constantly.

See also **Direction, strategic**; **End to end**; **Game, name of the**; **Pipedream**; **Road map**; **Stone, set in**

Plate, enough on one's

= phrase: a sufficiency

An unappetising meal.

Usage** – Dispirited junior and middle managers to their *colleagues* who, only half listening, counter with their own – much worse – story of woe.

See also **Colleague**; **Multitask**; **Time-poor**

Plate, step up to the

= phrase: accept a challenge

Beware the *curve ball*.

Usage**** – Managers using an Americanism (via the language of baseball) to try to make themselves sound decisive: '*We* need to stand up and be counted on this one. *You* need to *step up to the plate*.'

See also **Ball, curve**

Play, end of

= phrase: the conclusion of the day's business

Strictly speaking, five o'clock.

Usage* – Managers everywhere: 'Can you *ping* me that by *end of play* Friday?' Some po-faced executives use the acronyms

EOB (end of business) or COB (close of business) when setting a deadline.

See also **9–5**; **Ping**

Player
= n: an influential person

A charismatic individual. In a crowded room, follow the laughter in order to find him.

Usage ** – Directors with a wary respect for a business opponent; awed managers.

See also **A list**; **Bigwig**; **Cheese, big**; **Dickswinging**; **Fromage, grand**; **Heavyweight**; **Hitter, big**; **Shaker, mover and**

Plot, lose the
= phrase: to become angry; to lose direction

A misfortune if there is a complex narrative to be mastered.

Usage *** – Managers describing the all-too-typical behaviour of a *Sales manager* in a *meeting*: 'He *lost the plot*, big time, he did. *Threw his toys right out of the pram.*'

See also **Colleague**; **Meeting**; **Sales manager**; **Throw one's toys out of the pram**

Pockets, deep
= phrase: reserves of cash

A notable feature of corporate trousers.

Usage *** – Complacent Chairmen reflecting on the company's importance in the marketplace: 'We are a major *player* with *deep pockets.*'

See also **Global**; **Player**; **Right hand not knowing what the left hand is doing**; **Trouser**; **World-class**

Potato, hot

= n: a contentious subject

An item that should be handled very carefully, preferably by someone else.

Usage ** – *Unironic managers*; executives and senior managers with a *problem*; also managers who have successfully passed on a *problem* to an unsuspecting workmate; and managers who have just worked out why their hands are burning.

See also **Problem**; **Unironic manager**

Powwow

= n: a discussion or meeting

A ceremony used to prepare for conflict.

Usage ** – Managers of a certain age who have seen too many Randolph Scott[§] films: 'The big white chief is on the warpath. The smoke signals don't look good. We'd better get together for a *powwow*.'

See also **Huddle**; **Meeting**

[§] The square-jawed, inscrutable Randolph Scott played a series of leading roles in classic westerns in the 1940s and 1950s.

Practice, best

= n: the most effective method

The Holy Grail.

Usage ***** – An Offlish commonplace used by all kinds of manager in myriad circumstances.

See also **Improvement, continuous**

Pragmatic
= adj: practical; realistic

An overrated virtue. After all, every one of the world's most infamous dictators and tyrants could be said to have displayed this characteristic.

Usage** – Executives to the media, thereby signalling that they are capable of making the 'hard' decisions; in job adverts for a variety of positions, especially sales roles; candidates selling themselves at interviews: 'I like to be busy. I like to get things done. I'm something of a *pragmatist*' (translation: 'I don't have much up top, but if you have any bullying or sacking to do, then I'm your man').

See also **Axe**; **No-nonsense manager**; **Omelette, you have to crack eggs to make an**

Premiership English

A patois with depth, richness and rough poetry that is a refreshing influence on the language of Offlish. Noted experts in this fast-moving linguistic area are *Ron Atkinson*, *Alan Hansen* and John Motson.

See also **Age, come of**; **Ask, big**; **Ron Atkinson**; **Bouncebackability**; **Card, red**; **Class, different**; **Comics, reading too many**; **Corn, earn one's**; **Doors, early**; **Fantasy football**; **Feet, went in with both**; **Front, leading from the**; **Handbags**; **Alan Hansen**; **Journeyman**; **Mercurial**; **Pear-shaped, go**; **Percentages, play the**; **Professional, consummate**; **Stall, set out one's**

Pressure!, no
= phrase: don't worry

An invitation that is not what it seems.

Usage** – When you hear this phrase, inevitably used as a jokey exclamation by humourless executives, you have a choice. First, wherever you are, pick up your things, go back to your desk, collect your most important personal belongings and head for the exit. You may wish to say a swift and smiling goodbye to your workmates. In any event, like Lot escaping Sodom and Gomorrah, do not look back. This is not the place for you. Alternatively, chuckle along with everyone else and then knuckle down to a long life of corporate serfdom.

See also **Humour, sense of**

Principles, first
= n: fundamental laws or truths

These are rarely written down and, therefore, very difficult to locate in a crisis.

Usage**** – Bewildered executives reintroducing a '*back to basics*' programme from a supposedly golden age: 'In terms of the future, *going forward* we need to get back to *first principles*' (translation: 'Why don't we go back to what we all know best . . . and, ah, hope for the best . . .').

See also **Basics, back to**; **Core**; **Forward, going**; **Non-core**

Prioritize§
= v: to rank in importance

The answer to most questions.

Usage***** – Everyone, everywhere, constantly.

§ The addition of the suffix 'ize' to simple words to make them appear more complicated or important-sounding is common in Offlish: for example, 'potentialize', 'proceduralize', 'productize' or 'variabilize'.

Proactive

= adj: taking initiative; anticipating (rather than reacting)

A disposition that defines the premier law of management.

Usage ***** – For *Stephen R. Covey* this was the first of the seven habits to be acquired in order to be a highly effective person/manager. One of the most important Offlish principles, it is used by managers everywhere seeking to convey urgency about their humdrum tasks: 'We need to ask the right questions and be *proactive* on this one.' It is also used, for example, by *Ambitious managers* politically; by *Californian* and *Training managers* zealously; by *Sales managers* again-and-again-and-again; and by *Unironic managers* constantly. It also appears in job adverts for all kinds of roles and is, therefore, dutifully repeated by all kinds of candidates.

See also **Ambitious manager**; **Californian manager**; **Stephen R. Covey**; **Sales manager**; **Training manager**; **Unironic manager**

Problem

= n: a difficult situation requiring a solution

A predicament that can be solved in myriad ways.

Usage *** – For the *Ambitious manager*, always someone else's; for the *Californian manager* an '*opportunity*'; for the *Dramatic manager* a crisis; for the *Lackadaisical manager* a bore; for the *Life coach* an extension of their contract; for the *management consultant* a commission; for the *Micromanager* a lack of information; for the *PR manager* a story to be managed; for the *Sales manager* something to be hidden; for the *Training manager* a '*challenge*'; for the *Unironic manager* a chance to trot out the line (in a ludicrous American accent): 'Houston, we have a *problem*'; however, for the executive who prides himself on making the 'tough calls', it is 'something that can't be solved just by throwing money at it'.

See also **Ambitious manager**; **Californian manager**; **Challenge**; **Dramatic manager**; **Hiccup**; **Lackadaisical manager**;

Life coach; **Management consultant**; **Micromanager**;
Opportunity; **Potato, hot**; **Public Relations manager**;
Sales manager; **Unironic manager**

Professional, consummate
= n: an individual displaying a high level of competency

The highest accolade.

Usage*** – A phrase (via *Premiership English*, perhaps) often
used by managers to describe their *CEO* in the hope that the
compliment will, in a form of primitive magic, be redirected
back to themselves.

See also **CEO**; **Premiership English**

Prophecy
= n: a prophetic utterance; a prediction of future events

Invariably self-fulfilling.

Usage**** – *Unironic managers*.

See also **Unironic managers**

Punch one's weight
= phrase: to fight according to one's abilities

For those distrustful of the slipperiness of language, this
simple pugilistic trial – similar to the hammer-and-bell game
in fairgrounds – is a sure indicator of healthfulness.

Usage*** – Managers adopting a belligerent stance, especially
Sales and *No-nonsense managers*: 'To be fair we have turned
the corner, and with a fair wind we'll soon be *punching our
weight* again.'

See also **No-nonsense manager**; **Sales manager**

Public Relations manager

Perpetually cheery and positive, she (less often, he) nonetheless carries a great burden of trust and knowledge. An expert in spin and *hype*, she is a noisy exclaimer of official half-truths and partial revelations. She is a gushing gilder-of-the-lily; a hobnobber and small-talker of genius who is distrusted by everyone. She should, if at all possible, be avoided.

See also **A list, the**; **Armageddon**; **Black arts**; **Front, leading from the**; **Greenfield opportunity**; **Hearts and minds, winning**; **Problem**; **Reasons, personal**; **Scapegoat**; **Sex up**; **Sword, double-edged**; **Team, dream**; **Truth**

Puppet
= n: a person controlled by another

An individual who is linked to another person by powerful ties.

Usage* – Embittered managers who have been passed over for promotion.

See also **Yes-man**

Pussycat
= n: a feline

Even the most docile cat has claws. *Fat cats* are especially vicious once roused to a temper.

Usage* – Naive managers.

See also **Cat, fat**

Put one's head above the parapet
= phrase: to expose to danger

A perilous activity that is best left to others.

Usage *** – *Worldly-wise managers* offering advice to a callow protégé.

See also **Worldly-wise manager**

Python, mad as a writhing
= phrase: eccentric or unconventional

A startling sight.

Usage *** – Managers – originality being, more often than not, misunderstood – describing a (more successful) *colleague*. In the hurly-burly of the office it is useful to have a supply of 'mad as . . .' analogies.

See also **Bag of snakes, mad as a**; **Box of frogs, mad as a**; **Colleague**; **Fish, mad as a**; **Swing bin, mad as a**

Quality-driven
= adj: proficient

A mongrel term: the offspring of fashion and twaddle.

Usage ***** – Sardonic *management consultants*; unblushing executives who don't care if they are talking nonsense; pretentious, jargon-ridden job adverts written by empty-headed *HR managers*; eager-to-please candidates who hope that Offlish will make them appear in-the-club, businesslike, pliant and, therefore, suitable for corporate employment; on-the-make managers who use Offlish gobbledegook to show their seeming *commitment* to the cause; lazy managers who take refuge in Offlish rather than thinking for themselves; also *Unironic managers* who don't know any better. (A substitute expression is 'quality-focused'.)

See also **Commitment**; **Human Resources manager**; **Management consultant**; **Unironic manager**

Quid pro quo
= n: something given in compensation (Latin: 'something for something')

A popular company motto.

Usage **** – Senior managers, unfamiliar with Latin, outlining the latest tactical initiative: 'When all is said and done, we've had a *bumpy ride* recently and there is still a shortfall in *the numbers*. The *quid pro quo* is that, having explored all the options, we now have a handle on the *problem*' (translation: 'There will be no bonus this year, but there will be at least three months of unpaid overtime in order to achieve the reforecast').

See also **Numbers, the**; **Problem**; **Ride, bumpy**

Ramp up
= v: to increase or improve effort

An inclination that is not shared by all.

Usage **** – Managers everywhere, but especially *Sales managers* as a strapping version of 'doing better than last time': 'We need to get into gear and redouble our efforts on this one. We really need to *ramp it up*.' It is, however, mostly used more in hope than expectation. The *Unironic manager* will often add the threadbare tag: 'Hard work never hurt anyone.' [§] (A variation is 'ratchet up'.)

See also **Sales manager**; **Unironic manager**

[§] It was Ronald Reagan – famous for, among other things, his afternoon naps – who supposedly remarked: 'But I figure why take the chance?'

Reasons, personal

= phrase: a private justification

An explanation that cannot be gainsaid.

Usage*** – PR statements describing the departure of a board member. It is also used ironically by managers (often with the addition of inscribed-in-the-air inverted commas): 'He's left for "*personal reasons*". Just as well. He was neither use nor ornament.'

See also **Go, let**; **Public Relations manager**

Record

= n: evidence; a document or official report

Often speaks for itself.

Usage***** – *Unironic managers*.

See also **Track record**; **Unironic manager**

Respect, with all due

= phrase: showing esteem or deference

The correct preamble to launch a wild and savage attack.

Usage***** – Managers in *meetings* everywhere. (A common variation is 'with the greatest respect'.)

See also **Meeting**

Restructure

= v: to reallocate roles and responsibilities

A conjuring trick played on unwilling victims.

Usage**** – An Offlish euphemism for making redundancies, used by *CEOs* and executives to introduce the latest *strategic* stunt, which is always a variation of a better future brought about by fewer *people* doing more work for bigger profits.

See also **Asset**; **CEO**; **Defenestration**; **Downsize**; **Go, let**; **Losses, cut**; **People**; **Strategy**; **Wood, dead**

Results
= n: outcome; list of scores or winners

Usually open to interpretation.

Usage *** – Managers who have '*good news*'; *Marketing managers* airily; *Micromanagers* exhaustively; also in job adverts for sales positions: 'You will have demonstrated a strong orientation towards achieving *results*.' Executives are prone to demanding 'real *results*', while *No-nonsense managers* will state as an incontrovertible fact that it is 'not over until the fat lady sings' and agree with *Alan Hansen* on the essential point that 'the League table doesn't lie'.

See also **Bean counter**; **Alan Hansen**; **Marketing manager**; **Micromanager**; **No-nonsense manager**; **Numbers, the**

Results-focused
= adj: proficient

A mongrel term: the offspring of fashion and stupidity.

Usage ***** – Managers who describe themselves as '*entrepreneurial*'; unblushing executives who don't care if they are talking nonsense; pretentious, jargon-ridden job adverts written by empty-headed *HR managers*; eager-to-please candidates who hope that Offlish will make them appear in-the-club, businesslike, pliant and, therefore, suitable for corporate employment; on-the-make managers who use Offlish gobbledegook to show their seeming *commitment* to the cause; lazy managers who take refuge in Offlish rather than thinking for themselves; also *Unironic managers* who don't know any better.

See also **Commitment**; **Entrepreneur**; **Human Resources manager**; **Unironic manager**

Ride, bumpy

= phrase: difficult period

A journey that sometimes begins with a gentle oscillation but always ends with a violent shaking.

Usage** – A phrase used regularly by airline pilots and politicians, it is also used by uncaring senior managers euphemistically to describe an upcoming period of *change*: 'I'm afraid to say that it is likely we will be having a *bumpy ride* around the corner' (translation: 'I will ensure personally that you will *work like a navvy* for the foreseeable future').

See also **Change**; **Forward, going**; **Navvy, working like a**

Risk-averse

= adj: cautious behaviour

A state favoured by the watchful.

Usage**** – Senior managers and executives who believe that it makes them sound like a statesman (rather than a coward or procrastinator). It is used by the managers to stall for time: 'Until we know more, I'm inclined to be *risk-averse* on this one. I'd like to take a step back for a moment, look at the *big picture*, gather more information, pick a few brains, canvas some other opinions, and then come back with a more considered view' (translation: 'I've got no idea whatsoever about this. What do you think?').

See also **Percentages, play the**; **Picture, big**

Road map

= n: a map showing the roads of an area; a plan of action

An essential navigational tool for world leaders.

Usage*** – PR statements; also self-important managers for whom the office has all the drama and importance of major geopolitical negotiations with worldwide implications. It is

also used in pretentious job adverts for senior positions:
'You will deliver shareholder value through developing
a *road map* for future improvement initiatives.'

See also **Plan**

Robbing Peter to pay Paul
= proverb: to borrow from one source and give to another,
thereby creating another problem

A laborious but effective technique for balancing the books.

Usage** – Concerned executives: 'It's a merry-go-round is what
it is. We need to reprofile this expenditure. There's no point in
just *robbing Peter to pay Paul*'; grumpy managers; canny
Finance managers.

See also **Finance manager; Numbers, the**

Rock and a hard place, between a
= proverb: a choice between equally disadvantageous
alternatives

A familiar dilemma in the office.

Usage* – Resigned managers.

See also **Barrel, over a; Catch-22; Devil and the deep blue sea,
between the; Hobson's choice**

Rock and roll, let's
= phrase: let's rock and roll

An invitation that under no circumstances should be accepted.

Usage** – In an attempt to be simultaneously matey and
inspirational, middle-aged managers embarrassing themselves
in *meetings* in armpit-torching fashion: 'Let's *rock and roll*!'

See also **Inspirational; Meeting**

Rocket science

= n: a complex activity

A highly technical body of knowledge that has, alas, no profitable application in the office.

Usage ***** – Frequently used in exasperation by senior managers: 'Hey, *people*, this isn't *rocket science.*' It is also popular with *No-nonsense managers*, as they instinctively hate discussion of any kind (other than about sex, drinking and football); and *Ambitious managers* because it is the kind of phrase used by senior managers; and *Unironic managers* who never think about what they are saying.

See also **Ambitious manager**; **No-brainer**; **No-nonsense manager**; **People**; **Throw the baby out with the bath water, don't**; **Unironic manager**

Rome wasn't built in a day

= proverb: 'Achievements of great pith and moment are not accomplished without patience and perseverance and a considerable interval of time' (*Brewer's Dictionary of Phrase and Fable*)

An unquestionable historical fact.

Usage * – *Lackadaisical managers* casually explaining away their dilatoriness; *Worldly-wise managers* reiterating a great truth.

See also **Lackadaisical manager**; **Mañana**; **Worldly-wise manager**

Ropes, on the

= phrase: a desperate position

A place where savage punishment is administered.§

Usage* – Under-fire managers. The influence of the noble art of boxing in the office has been generally underestimated.

See also **Diving, ducking and**; **Knockout blow**

§ The rope-a-dope worked for Muhammad Ali in the 'Rumble in the Jungle' against George Foreman in 1975 – but he was The Greatest.

Roundabouts, swings and
= phrase: a situation where there are no gains or losses

A modern version of ancient wisdom such as yin and yang or karma.

Usage *** – Pontificating *Worldly-wise managers*, and managers breezily attempting to gloss over a personal blunder: 'It'll come out in the wash. It's a *swings and roundabouts* situation' (translation: 'I'm almost certain that I can cover this up').

See also **Worldly-wise manager**

Rule of thumb
= n: guidance based on experience

A traditional system of thought that is efficacious in the majority of situations.

Usage ** – For different reasons, *Lackadaisical* and *Worldly-wise managers* regularly; and *No-nonsense managers* because anything else is just 'fannying around'.

See also **Lackadaisical manager**; **No-nonsense manager**; **Worldly-wise manager**

Sacred cow
= n: exempt from criticism; something that cannot be questioned

An extinct species.

Usage ** – 'Today, there are no *sacred cows*': *gurus* advancing an argument that allows them to peddle any old nonsense as intelligent speculation; *management consultants* hustling for business; executives extolling the relentless *changeability* of the market to show their intellectual broad-mindedness (and to get their excuses in early).

See also **Change**; **Guru**; **Management consultant**

Sales manager

Fierce and muleish, he likes everyone to know that he is someone who 'speaks his mind'. He is the self-appointed 'lifeblood' of the company, as well as its '*eyes and ears*', since he is the person who talks to customers directly (albeit as little as possible). His sleeves are always '*rolled up*', he has his '*finger on the pulse*'. A great opponent of 'window dressing', he is unlikely 'to take a back seat' and will insist on 'calling the shots'. A finger-wagger and desk-pounder, he enjoys nothing better than a barney. (In fact, it is often said by his colleagues that he could start an argument in an empty room.) He has a perpetual frown and is often seen stomping down corridors while shouting commands or abuse. He also has many strong views on other departments and, exhaustively, the company car policy. He loathes everybody, is loathed by everybody, and he should, if at all possible, be avoided.[§]

See also **Act together, get our**; **Assertive**; **Attitude, can-do**; **Balls**; **Basics, back to**; **Behind, get**; **Bung**; **Coal face, at the**; **Curlies, short and**; **Customer-facing**; **Doomsday scenario**; **Drive**; **Drum, bang the**; **Excellence, centre of**; **Eyes and ears**; **Finger on the pulse**; **Firing on all cylinders**; **Gas, cooking with**; **Growth, explosive**; **Humour, sense of**; **Liar**; **Plot, lose the**; **Problem**; **Punch one's weight**; **Ramp up**; **Sharp end, at the**; **Sleeves**; **Smoke and mirrors**; **Stack up**; **Street cred**; **Talk**; **Thinking, lateral**; **Trenches, in the**; **Up for it?**; **What's what**; **Whistles, bells and**; **Word on the street**

[§] The collective noun for *Sales managers* is a conviction.

Saloon, the last chance
= n: a final opportunity

A popular drinking hole.

Usage *** – Managers delighting in the imminent downfall of a *colleague*.

See also **Colleague**

Samurai manager

Bellicose and proud, he is a terrifying sight when roused to action. For him the office is life-and-death warfare. His vocabulary is martial, his *team* are warriors, and while ritual suicide is an option, failure is not. *Sun Tzu's The Art of War* is his manual; his governing code is *bushido*, emphasising loyalty, bravery and endurance. His steadfastness to his master is unquestioned; however, unless you are prepared to don armour and wield a sword, he should, if at all possible, be avoided.[§]

See also **Chest, war**; **Colours**; **Front, leading from the**; **Sun Tzu**; **Sword, double-edged**; **Take no prisoners**; **Trenches, in the**; **Troops, the**; **War zone**

[§] The collective noun for *Samurai managers* is a phalanx.

Sanity check
= n: a final overview

To the mad it is everyone else who is insane.

Usage ** – Woebegone managers everywhere of a last-minute review undertaken by a senior manager irrespective of the fact that he may be mad as a . . . (please supply suitable analogy). *Unironic managers* will *always* add the catchphrase: 'You don't have to be mad to work here – but it helps.'

See also **Box of frogs, mad as a**; **Eleventh hour, at the**; **Fish, mad as a**; **Python, mad as a writhing**; **Swing bin, mad as a**; **Unironic manager**

Scapegoat
= n: a sacrifice

A useful animal to have tethered in a prominent spot in the office.

Usage* – Bewildered managers who have been cast out; relieved managers who have seen peers cast out. Also *PR managers*, privately, who have a difficult story to manage.

See also **Lamb, sacrificial**; **Public Relations manager**; **Team**; **Upwards, managing**

Scatter-gun
= n: a shotgun

An effective weapon, if lacking in precision.

Usage** – Managers describing the company's latest initiative: 'It's the usual *scatter-gun* approach; let's *throw* some *mud at the wall* and see what sticks.'

See also **Put one's head above the parapet**; **Shoot oneself in the foot**; **Throw mud at the wall**

Scenario, best case
= phrase: the most favourable outcome

A rare event.

Usage***** – Managers in *meetings* followed immediately by 'but . . .' and a long and tedious narrative explaining why it is unlikely to occur; journalists presenting an alternative version of the official corporate PR story.

See also **Meeting**

Self-starter
= n: an ambitious, self-motivated person

A widely admired type – especially among *self-starters*.

Usage *** – Job-seekers in application letters and *CVs*; also in job adverts and interviews, especially for sales positions, where it roughly translates as: 'You're on your own. Your manager will not speak to you. Your colleagues will not speak to you (unless it is to check that your salary is lower than theirs). It's *sink or swim*, mate.'

See also **CV**; **Sink or swim**

Self-toast
= v: to incriminate oneself

A word of warning: the office can be a dangerous place.

Usage **** – Rueful managers reflecting on an unfortunate faux pas: '. . . It could have happened to anyone. Just one word out of place, but it was too late. I'd *self-toasted*.' The most effective way to avoid this experience is to say as little as possible in *meetings*. As a result you may get a reputation as a renowned conciliator and deep thinker or, alternatively, as a shy, know-nothing wallflower. Either way, happily, everyone will keep their distance.

See also **Meeting**

Sex up
= v: to augment

It is widely accepted that the majority of reports and

presentations require a little something to add interest and piquancy. It is, after all, impolite to bore your audience.

Usage **** – Executives and *PR managers* privately; managers forgetting for a moment that they are not on *Newsnight* or the *Today* programme.

See also **Public Relations manager**

Shaker, mover and
= n: an influential person

A *player*.

Usage** – Directors with a wary respect for a business opponent; awed managers.

See also **Cheese, big**; **Dickswinging**; **Fromage, grand**; **Heavyweight**; **Hitter, big**; **Player**

Shambles
= n: a mess or muddle; a place of carnage

The inevitable result of the intervention of a *colleague*.

Usage **** – Managers everywhere.

See also **Balls-up**; **Colleague**

Sharp end, at the
= phrase: dealing with customers

A posting that should be resisted with great vigour.

Usage ** – *Sales managers* who believe that because they occasionally speak to customers they are the *only* people who really know what is happening in the company.

See also **Coal face, at the**; **Eyes and ears**; **Sales manager**; **What's what**

Shoot oneself in the foot
= phrase: self-administered accident

Sadly, this is a common misadventure in the office.

Usage *** – Managers celebrating a *colleague*'s calamity or, out of hearing of their boss, the latest corporate howler.

See also **Colleague**; **Goal, own**; **Self-toast**

Shoots, green
= n: evidence of growth

A heartening sight, even if they often fail to come to fruition.

Usage ** – Chairmen and PR statements pointing to an imminent recovery in sales, profits and share prices; also managers who have nothing concrete to present but who recognise that they can at least sound positive.

See also **News, good**

Shop, talking
= n: a forum

A useful place to barter and exchange views.

Usage ** – *No-nonsense managers* dismissing the *meeting* they have just left as they walk down the corridor to their next *meeting*: 'Yak, yak, yak. Fiddling while Rome burns. Talk about *rearranging the deckchairs on the Titanic*'; *Ambitious managers* agreeing vehemently – '*Absolutely!*' – with the judgement of a senior manager.

See also **Absolutely!**; **Ambitious manager**; **Meeting**; **No-nonsense manager**; **Titanic, rearranging the deckchairs on the**

Show, dog and pony
= n: a presentation

A spectacle that often proves a disappointment.

Usage ** – Senior managers describing an important presentation. Please note that this must never be interpreted literally.

See also **Tongues, speaking in**

SUMO
= acronym: Shut Up and Move On

Excellent advice.

Usage **** – Managers and executives who have grown far, far too fond of their own voices.

See also **Meeting**

Sickie
= n: a period of sick leave

Time given over to necessary rest and private reflection.

Usage ** – A 'duvet day' (or days, depending on the severity of the need) set aside for the proper rest and recuperation of the enfeebled worker. Formerly known as St Monday, this is an ancient folk tradition that deserves enthusiastic patronage in order to survive in the modern world. The term is used derogatively by managers who know the truth but cannot prove it: 'I got a message on the answerphone. The bastard's taken another *sickie*.'[§]

See also **Home, working from**

[§] Appendix Three – The Sickie: Planning and Implementation

Sink or swim
= phrase: either success or failure

An age-old test of an individual's capacity to learn quickly.

Usage ** – New starters complaining about their 30-minute

induction, in which some nitwit from the HR department took them round the building showing them fire exits and toilets, introduced them to lots of people, most of whom they will never see again, and then left them at a desk with an enormous in-tray; also *No-nonsense managers* approvingly:'I didn't get where I am today by being mollycoddled.[§] *Sink or swim.*That will soon sort out the men from the boys.'

See also **No-nonsense manager**

[§] CJ, the oracular boss in the Reginald Perrin series, left a set of memorable sayings that continue to inspire the *No-nonsense manager*, such as:'I didn't get where I am today by...
...making room for broken reeds, lame ducks or stool pigeons.'
...looking a gift horse in the mouth. Or by going down with
  a sinking ship.'
...pouring cold water over a wet blanket.'
...without striking while the bird in the hand is hot.'
...apologising.'

Sit on the fence
= phrase: to prevaricate

Not a comfortable spot on which to perch, but it does afford a good view.

Usage** - Managers among their peers accusing their boss of political cowardice or chicanery:'He's been *sitting on the fence* for so long he must have calluses on his backside.'

See also **Balls**; **Cojones**

Sit-down
= n: a conference

One of the most common requests in the office, yet still one of the most alarming.

Usage**** - Managers requesting a *meeting* with a subordinate:

'We need a *sit-down*' (translation: '*I* need to talk at you. Do *not* interrupt. *You* need to listen to what I have to say. This is very important to *me*. At the end of this monologue you will go away and do everything *I* have told you to do').

See also **Meeting**

Situation, no win
= phrase: guaranteed defeat or failure

But it's the taking part that's important, isn't it?

Usage**** - Executives privately throwing in the towel; weary or stoical managers who know that there is nothing that can be done; *Californian managers* in a sweat of anxiety.

See also **Californian manager**

Skill set
= n: abilities

An important package where, as elsewhere, size matters.

Usage**** - Cynical *HR managers* and numskull *Training managers*; in job adverts for a variety of positions: 'Your *skill set* will be varied. You will *challenge* norms by *thinking laterally*. You will be an *influencer* as well as an implementer, and you will enjoy working in a climate in which people are mutually enabling and collaborative' (translation: 'We are looking for a combination of Richard Branson and Judy Finnegan. Is that how you see yourself?').

See also **Challenge**; **Human Resources manager**; **Influencer**; **Interpersonal**; **Thinking, lateral**; **Training manager**

Slave driver
= n: a person who works others very hard

An individual with a clear ethical code.

Usage** – Downtrodden managers everywhere:'It's non-stop. I'm *working like a Trojan*. He's a *slave driver*.'

See also **CrackBerry; Trojan, working like a**

Sledgehammer to crack a nut
= phrase: to use a lot of effort to solve a small problem

Messy – but it does get the job done every time.

Usage* – A disbelieving colleague of the *No-nonsense manager*'s approach to problem-solving.

See also **No-nonsense manager**

Sleeves
= n: that part of a garment which covers the arms

Offlish etiquette requires that these should be rolled up at all times.

Usage*** – *Sales managers* habitually; job adverts for sales positions that proudly proclaim a '*sleeves*-rolled-up culture'; candidates recommending themselves.

See also **Sales manager**

Smoke and mirrors
= n: misleading information

A variation on *son et lumière* shows.

Usage*** – A Chairman's rebuttal to the media of a potential takeover or boardroom coup:'*At this moment in time* I can confirm that there's nothing in these rumours. It's all just *smoke and mirrors*' (translation:'By tomorrow, of course, everything may have changed and I could be sitting pretty with my share options'); managers dismissing a proposal that, if implemented, would put them at a disadvantage; managers suspecting a plot against them. It is also used by *No-nonsense* and *Sales managers* to dismiss anything to do with either the Brand or Marketing departments.

See also **Machiavellian manager**; **No-nonsense manager**; **Sales manager**; **Time, at this moment in**

Snake in the grass
= phrase: a treacherous person; secret enemy

Watch your step: the office can be a dangerous place.

Usage* – Managers complaining, usually without any concrete evidence, about the underhand political manoeuvring of a (more successful) *colleague*.

See also **Colleague**; **Machiavellian manager**

Space, watch this
= phrase: await developments

An activity that usually yields only small rewards.

Usage***** – Executives briefing the press (translation:'. . . possibly for a very long time. . .'); smug managers. It is also a phrase popular with *Unironic managers* who believe, erroneously, that this will add a dash of invigorating suspense to any conversation or presentation.

See also **Cracks, papering over the**; **Lips, read my**

Space cadet
= n: a scatterbrain

In the office there is a place for everyone.

Usage* – Managers mocking a *colleague* (or *'airhead'*) whose powers of disorganisation are a constant source of amusement and encouragement.

See also **Airhead**; **Colleague**; **Muppet**

Speed, up to
= phrase: to be informed

A perpetual undertaking and a philosophical conundrum. Despite the ever-increasing pace of office life and the vast amount of time devoted to this issue, the end goal is never reached. In this respect it is reminiscent of one of Zeno's paradoxes.[§]

Usage ***** – Managers everywhere, but especially the *Micromanager*.

See also **Micromanager**

[§] Zeno of Citium was a Greek philosopher in the 5th century BC whose paradoxes questioned the evidence of the senses: for example, the paradox of Achilles and the tortoise where he argued that Achilles, once he had given the tortoise a head start, could never catch it up since, when he arrived where it had been, it had already moved forwards; or the paradox of the arrow that can never reach its target.

Square, thinking outside the
= phrase: having innovative ideas

Usage ***** – Central to the self-image of the *Brand* and *Marketing manager*, but also used often by anyone who likes to present themselves as unconventional and *inspirational*. It is also regularly seen in job adverts for creative roles and often demanded by managers in response to all kinds of *problems*, yet is rarely acted on: 'We need to go beyond the conventional wisdom and *think outside the square*.'

See also **Box, thinking outside the**; **Brand manager**;
Inspirational; **Marketing manager**; **Off-the-wall**; **Problem**;
Unthinkable, thinking the

Square peg in a round hole
= phrase: ill-fitting; ill-suited

A situation that inevitably results in a good deal of effortful
pushing and pulling.

Usage** – Cynical *HR managers* briskly dismissing a former
colleague's career.

See also **Colleague**; **Human Resources manager**

Squeaky-clean
= adj: spotless; guiltless

A wholesome sound and a dazzling sight.

Usage** – Managers encouraging their subordinates to complete
a task in a particular way in order to avoid incurring the
displeasure of their superiors: 'We need to be *squeaky-clean* on
this one, *guys*. We have to be whiter than white. *Comprendez?*'

See also **Guys**

Stack up
= v: to add up to a total

A phrase, usually a question, of great import and forensic
concentration. It should not be used in jest.

Usage*** – Often used when debating *the numbers* and
assessing '*the bottom line*' – as a hopeful question from an
executive: 'This does *stack up?*'; as a straightforward assertion
from a *Finance manager*: 'This just doesn't *stack up*'; as a
blunt cross-examination from a *Sales manager*: 'How will
this *stack up?*'; and as a diversionary tactic from the

Ambitious manager: 'Does this really *stack up?*'

See also **Ambitious manager**; **Bottom line, the**;
Finance manager; **Numbers, the**; **Sales manager**

Stakhanovite, working like a

= phrase: exceptionally industrious (A. G. Stakhanov, 1906-77,
was a miner who in 1935 produced a record-breaking amount
of coal in a day and became an exemplar for the Soviet state
and people)

A state of self-pity brought about by a period of sustained heroic
achievement that has gone unrecognised and unrewarded.

Usage* – *Thesaurus managers*, with a what-can-I-do grimace
(translation: 'Therefore, can I suggest you shove it where the
sun doesn't shine?'). It is useful in the office to have a supply of
'working like a . . .' analogies.

See also **Dog, working like a**; **Navvy, working like a**;
Thesaurus manager; **Trojan, working like a**

Stall, set out one's

= phrase: demonstrate one's mettle

A noisy and time-consuming activity that can wreck a *meeting*
before it properly begins.

Usage** – *No-nonsense managers* adopting *Premiership
English* to make a point. This can take some time.

See also **Doors, early**; **Meeting**; **No-nonsense manager**;
Premiership English

State of the art

= n: the most advanced technology

Today's finest – and soon to be yesterday's – technology.

Usage*** – It is used by *IT managers* habitually: 'It's cutting-edge *state of the art*'; as well as executives puffing a new product or service (translation: 'This is the best we could afford while still enabling us to make our usual handsome profit'), directors announcing a new project and senior managers repeating the company line.

See also **Leading-edge**; **IT manager**

Stick, carrot and
= phrase: threats and incentives

An effective method of encouragement – for donkeys.

Usage *** – *No-nonsense managers* (with a striking emphasis on the *stick* rather than the *carrot*).

See also **No-nonsense manager**

Stone, set in
= phrase: fixed

A position best avoided, as alterations thereafter will be difficult and costly.

Usage ** – Managers carefully avoiding a concrete proposal that might at some point in the future leave them '*holding the can*'.

See also **Can, holding the**; **Plan**

Stops, the
= n: part of an organ

Invariably pulled out.

Usage *** – *Unironic managers* exhorting their *team* to the maximum effort: 'We need to pull out all *the stops* on this one, *guys*.'

See also **Guys**; **Mile, go the extra**; **Team**; **Unironic manager**

Story, sob

= n: an explanation appealing to the emotions

A tale guaranteed to bring a tear to the eye.

Usage** – Managers privately exulting in a *colleague*'s discomfort over a mistake or blunder.

See also **Colleague**

Strategy

= n: long-term plan of action; the art of war

The sum of day-to-day tactics.

Usage***** – For the *CEO* a script; for the board a mantra; for senior managers a grinding labour; for middle and junior managers a mystery; for everyone else an irrelevance.

See also **Basics, back to**; **Bed in**; **Cat, fat**; **Charlatan**; **CEO**; **Consumer agenda**; **Competitive advantage**; **Core**; **Cracks, papering over the**; **Customer behaviour, changing**; **Customer-facing**; **Direction, strategic**; **Downsize**; **Drive**; **Fag packet, back of a**; **Game, name of the**; **Global**; **Greenfield opportunity**; **Hat**; **Hiccup**; **Hindsight**; **Jerry-built**; **Improvement, continuous**; **Long haul, in for the**; **Losses, cut**; **Non-core**; **Picture, big**; **Pipedream**; **Plan**; **Punch one's weight**; **Tweak**; **U-turn**; **World, brave new**

Street, two-way

= n: allowing traffic in either direction

Often closed or restricted to one-way traffic.

Usage**** – Senior managers who want to be seen as everyone's friend: 'I'm here. I'm available. My *door* is always *open*. This is a *two-way street*.'

See also **Door, open**

Street cred

= n: experience; know-how

It is always a mistake to attempt to demonstrate this in the office or, perhaps, anywhere else.

Usage** – *Sales managers* whose belief in the concept is unshakeable.

See also **Sales manager**; **Word on the street**

Strike, pre-emptive

= n: an advantage gained by attacking first

A bold and decisive act employed by bold and decisive individuals.

Usage*** – A term originally meaning the seizure of land and used in the modern context of 'smart' warfare to signify acting in an unscrupulous or hostile manner in order to secure an advantage. Any manager using military terminology is likely to be, at best, untrustworthy or, more probably, deranged. He should therefore, if at all possible, be avoided.

See also **Samurai manager**

Struggle

= n: a strenuous effort

Invariably uphill.

Usage* – *Unironic managers*.

See also **Unironic manager**

Sub-optimal

= adj: less than a total success

A common species of triumph over adversity.

Usage ***** – Managers beautifying the unlovely: '*To be honest*, implementation was *sub-optimal* and resulted in unexpected losses, but in the circumstances was a decent *result*' (translation: 'This was a complete disaster. We've lost shed loads'). Had Napoleon had the resources of Offlish at his disposal he might, for example, have referred to the march on Moscow as 'something of a *sub-optimal* experience that presented good *learnings going forward*'.

See also **Forward, going**; **Honest, to be**; **Learnings**; **Results**; **Tits up**

Succession planning
= n: a long-term plan for filling managerial vacancies

A system of considerable complexity and nuanced judgements.

Usage ** – Cynical *HR* managers: 'Our position is clear. Integrated *succession planning* is an essential part of our *people* process to *drive* a raft of benefits for the company and its shareholders' (translation: 'Hands up who has been here the longest/causes the least problems/will accept the lowest salary?').

See also **Drive**; **Human Resources manager**; **Meritocracy**; **Musical chairs**; **People**

Sucker
= n: a foolish person

In the office there is a place for everyone.

Usage ** – Managers adopting an outdated Hollywood tough-guy argot to describe a (more successful) *colleague*.

See also **Colleague**; **Loser**

Surprises, policy of no
= phrase: a code of openness

It can come as no surprise that this is rarely effective.

Usage* – Cynical *HR managers*: 'Our appraisal process operates
on a transparent *policy of no surprises* basis'; head-in-the-clouds
Californian managers; gobsmacked managers.

See also **Californian manager**; **Human Resources manager**

Sweetener
= n: a gift or incentive

An hallucinogenic substance that transforms an individual's
apprehension of reality.

Usage** – Contented executives, privately; grumbling managers.

See also **Bung**; **Handcuffs, golden**; **Hello, golden**

Swing bin, mad as a
= phrase: eccentric or unconventional

A striking sight.

Usage*** – Managers – originality being, more often than not, misunderstood – describing a (more successful) *colleague*. In the hurly-burly of the office it is useful to have a supply of 'mad as . . .' analogies.

See also **Bag of snakes, mad as a**; **Box of frogs, mad as a**; **Colleague**; **Fish, mad as a**; **Python, mad as a writhing**

Sword, double-edged
= n: an event with an ambiguous outcome

A popular weapon in the office.

Usage *** – Duplicitous *PR managers* spinning information; *Ambitious managers* unwilling to commit to a firm opinion in case it disadvantages them at a later date; *Worldly-wise managers* habitually, with a sage nod of the head; flailing managers who have not a clue as to the right answer.

See also **Ambitious manager**; **Flip side**; **Public Relations manager**; **Worldly-wise manager**

Synergy
= n: combined or co-ordinated action

A trick that, if performed confidently, sometimes astonishes the audience.

Usage **** – A high-sounding term that for many executives is an obsession, as they believe it makes them appear simultaneously intelligent, dynamic and up to date: 'We are maximising *synergies* in order to foster growth and deliver true *competitive advantage* to *drive* shareholder value' (translation: 'This sounds great, doesn't it? What's not to like?'). A flexible term, often used in connection with a reorganisation or *restructure*, it may also be used as an adjective – 'synergistic' – or as a verb – 'synergize'. The bestselling *Stephen R. Covey* has demonstrated that one of the characteristics of effective managers is that they are always 'synergizing'.

See also **Competitive advantage**; **Stephen R. Covey**; **Drive**; **Holistic**; **Restructure**; **Strategy**

Ts and Cs
= n: terms and conditions

An excellent hiding place.

Usage** – Shrewd corporate lawyers; obsessive *Micromanagers* who pile detail on detail and always insist that 'the Is are dotted and the Ts are crossed'.

See also **Micromanager**

Tacks, brass
= n: fundamental details

A vital stage of any discussion, debate or negotiation.

Usage* – Impatient *Sales managers*.

See also **Sales manager**

Take no prisoners
= phrase: to be ruthless

An injunction that at least has the considerable merits of precision and conciseness.

Usage*** – *Samurai managers* stating what is, for them, an unbreakable rule of office warfare: '*Team*, we need to get amongst them, *take no prisoners* and bring home the bacon.'

See also **Samurai manager**; **Team**

Take that on board
= phrase: to accept a point or argument

More honoured in the breach.

Usage**** – Managers everywhere in *meetings* as the
conventional method for agreeing to disagree: 'Yes. I hear
what you're saying. I *take that on board*' (translation: 'Wrong.
Wrong. Wrong. Wrong. Wrong').

See also **Meeting**

Talent, pool of

= phrase: persons of high ability

Unfortunately, in certain conditions, this can evaporate
very quickly.

Usage*** – *CEOs* at the company conference trotting
out the '*people* are our greatest *asset*' formula to reassure the
workforce that the company has 'a huge *pool of talent* to
draw on' while encouraging them to carry on 'demonstrating
extraordinary *commitment* to delivering the very
highest standards' (translation: 'Stick at it and, if you're
lucky, you might not be the first to lose your job in the
next *restructure*').

See also **Asset**; **CEO**; **Commitment**; **Downsize**; **People**;
Restructure; **Wood, dead**

Talk

= v & n: to communicate; a conversation

Often cheap.

Usage* – *Sales managers* demanding action; *Worldly-wise
managers* summarising an unsuccessful *meeting*.

See also **Feedback**; **Input**; **Meeting**; **Sales manager**;
Worldly-wise manager

Talk until blue in the face

= phrase: ineffective communication

A distressing sight. The knowledge of even basic first aid can be a lifesaver in certain circumstances.

Usage** – Self-righteous managers (a very large group) in a *meeting* who wish that 'PEOPLE. WOULD. JUST. STOP. AND. LISTEN.' Fortunately the discomfort is temporary, as there is always another *meeting* to go to.

See also **Meeting**

Teach your grandmother to suck eggs, don't
= proverb: to offer advice or assistance unnecessarily

The injunction remains popular, even though the custom has largely fallen into disuse.

Usage** – The introductory matter to a long-winded and unrequired explanation or tedious homily. It is particularly popular with *Worldly-wise managers*.

See also **Worldly-wise manager**

Team
= n: persons acting together for a common purpose

A collection of individuals situated in the same place at the same time.

Usage***** – Everyone, everywhere, endlessly.

See also **Act together, get our; Aligned; Cocks on the block; Collegiate; Ducks in a row; Firing on all cylinders; Happen, make it; Hit the ground running; Mile, go the extra; Motivation; Party, working; Passion; Scapegoat; Stops, the; Thinking, joined-up; Troops; Wavelength, on the same**

Team, catalyst
= n: a group charged with solving a problem

An ensemble that is guaranteed to get a reaction.

Usage** – Senior managers who don't know what to do next; *HR managers* who have recently been on a *Change* Management course; also *Ambitious managers* who learned nothing from the same course but recognise a chance to show off the latest Offlish jargon: 'Let's get a *catalyst team* together, scope the *opportunities* and make a *road map* for the future.'

See also **Ambitious manager**; **Change**; **Human Resources manager**; **Opportunity**; **Road map**; **Team**

Team, dream
= n: the best possible team

A fantasy.

Usage*** – *CEOs* and *PR managers* announcing the end of their recruitment search for '*the final piece of the jigsaw*'.

See also **CEO**; **Jigsaw, final piece of the**; **Public Relations manager**

Team player
= n: an unselfish person

An individual with an unusual ability, but one who is unlikely to progress up the *ladder*.

Usage*** – Managers who have little positive to say in an appraisal: 'Um ... Er ... You're a ... good ... *team player*' (translation: 'You are a time server who is unable to think for himself. You would be well advised to sort out your *CV*'). It also recurs in job adverts for customer service positions: 'You will be a *team player* comfortable operating in a multi-stakeholder environment where a daily balance must be struck between consensus and *action*' (translation: 'Could you get that phone! It's been ringing for ages').

See also **Action**; **CV**; **Ladder**; **Team**

Thesaurus manager

A long-winded disgorger of words. He believes that
plain-speaking often reveals plain-thinking and sees himself
as a veritable cornucopia or gallimaufry of wisdom. Look
out for an oversized dictionary and assorted miscellanies
and books of lists in his office. He will never use a short
word where a long, obscure word is available, or an English
word where there is an approximate foreign equivalent; he
is fond of quoting from classic literature (whether or not
the occasion is suitable and whether or not the quotation
is accurate) and is happy to pass on his threadbare
knowledge at any time. He is also a devotee of all the latest
intellectual crazes such as chaos theory or *tipping points*.
He is detested by everyone and should, if at all possible,
be avoided.[§]

See also **Bête noire**; **Catch-22**; **Defenestration**; **DNA**;
Draconian; **80/20 rule**; **Fromage, grand**; **Humour, sense
of**; **Overview**; **Stakhanovite, working like a**; **Tipping
point**; **Tour d'horizon**; **World, brave new**

[§] The collective noun for *Thesaurus managers* is a concordance.

Things, bigger and better
= phrase: an improved situation

Life, it has been said, is a journey with many twists and turns.

Usage ** – Managers giving their reasons for leaving their present
employment.

See also **Downsize**; **Go, let**; **Order of the boot**; **Out, up or**;
Reasons, personal; **Restructure**

Thinking, blue-sky

= n: experimental or innovative ideas

Play – fun, free and fruitless; the adult equivalent of children making block towers or splatter paintings.

Usage ***** – *Brand* and *Marketing managers* habitually; managers who see themselves as 'creative'; managers who don't know what to do next; also in job adverts for marketing positions: 'We don't believe in *sticking to the knitting*. We are looking for *out-of-the-box blue-sky thinking*' (translation: 'We are so desperate that any idea, no matter how daft and irrational, will be welcomed warmly . . .'). This phrase is now so common that many speakers inscribe inverted commas in the air to signify its classic Offlish status. Do not be tempted to follow their example.

See also **Blank canvas**; **Box, thinking outside the**; **Brand manager**; **Knitting, stick to the**; **Marketing manager**; **Off-the-wall**; **Square, thinking outside the**; **Tipping point**; **Unthinkable, thinking the**; **Vision**; **World, brave new**

Thinking, joined-up

= n: demonstrating unity; producing a coherent whole

A thing of beauty glimpsed only occasionally. For some, never experienced directly.

Usage ***** – A corporate mantra for managers everywhere; the answer to all *problems*: 'We need to see some *joined-up thinking* on this one. Let's get our *ducks in a row*.'

See also **Ducks in a row**; **Team**; **Wavelength, on the same**

Thinking, lateral

= n: examination of a problem from an unorthodox point of view

An uncommon commodity that is, in any event, often dismissed as worthless.

Usage *** – In job adverts for senior positions;[§] candidates at interviews repeating the advert; managers everywhere pleading for some kind of an answer. It is also used habitually by self-advertising *Brand* and *Marketing managers* who are confident that they have the answer. *No-nonsense* and *Sales managers* will, however, have no truck with it.

See also **Box, thinking outside the**; **Brand manager**; **Marketing manager**; **No-nonsense manager**; **Off-the-wall**; **Sales manager**; **Square, thinking outside the**

[§] 'Forward thinking' is a common variation; and on occasions the risible 'precision thinking' is used.

Throw mud at the wall
= phrase: a scattershot approach

The aim of this exercise is to discover what adheres and what falls to the floor. Unsurprisingly, this is a very messy business.

Usage *** – Managers, privately, describing the company's latest tactical initiative. *No-nonsense managers* prefer the scatological version of the phrase.

See also **No-nonsense manager**; **Scatter-gun**

Throw one's toys out of the pram
= phrase: to have a tantrum

For some, childhood spontaneity is a knack carried over into adulthood.

Usage **** – As with an errant two-year-old, a hissy fit is best ignored; however, if the toys belong to an executive or senior manager, then it is politic to return the rattles, teddy bears and soft, satin-edged blankets as quickly as possible: 'You should have seen him. Shouting and bawling. *Threw his toys right out of the pram.*'

See also **Grown-up**; **Plot, lose the**

Throw the baby out with the bath water, don't
= phrase: don't lose the essential

Advice considered unnecessary by doctors and midwives.

Usage **** – *Brand managers* who are perpetually anxious about the wellbeing of the '*brand* baby'; cautious senior managers in *meetings*; also *Unironic managers* for whom the obvious is always worth underlining.

See also **Brand**; **Brand manager**; **Meeting**; **Rocket science**; **Unironic manager**

Thumbs-down
= n: an indication of failure or dissatisfaction

An ancient and universally recognised sign.

Usage * – Managers in *meetings*, as the gesture is as well understood in the office as it was originally by Romans and gladiators.

See also **Meeting**

Tick in the box
= phrase: a mark used to indicate approval; something checked or dealt with

Usage ***** – One of the most popular and stupid Offlish expressions, it is used in many different contexts – and often shortened to a single exuberant 'Tick!' – to register that the relevant manager has approved an activity or piece of work. Like so much Offlish usage, this is not a phrase one would ever use outside work, or if you do, gentle reader, then either you are hopelessly baffled by this book or you have already thrown it across the room in exasperation.

See also **Bed, put to**; **Ducks in a row**; **Green light**; **Hoops, jump through the**; **Unironic manager**

Till, hand in the
= phrase: thievery; stealing

An illegal act (but one which, in cases of fraud, can be very difficult to prove).

Usage *** – Tabloid journalists covering a corporate imbroglio and getting to the essentials of the story; senior managers revelling in the corporate fallout: 'They've been caught with their *hands in the till* this time all right. Heads will roll. Mark my words' (translation: 'What's in it for me?').

Time, at this moment in
= phrase: now

The correct formula to preface any (self-)important statement.

Usage ***** – Pompous executives and managers in *meetings* and presentations everywhere. 'At this point in time' is a common variation.

See also **Meeting**

Time-poor
= adj: lacking leisure time

A deeply distressing and discomforting psychological state that is a direct result of employment.

Usage **** – Exhausted managers catching up with emails and work-related reading at the weekends. Sufferers are inclined to irritableness, rudeness and self-questioning of an existential nature such as: 'What does it all mean?' or 'Is this all there is?'

See also **Monday to Friday**; **9-5**; **Plate, enough on one's**; **Time-rich**

Time-rich
= adj: having leisure time

A state of happiness that is not consistent with paid employment.

Usage**** – Retired managers.

See also **Time-poor**

Tin, does what it says on the
= phrase: straightforward; unambiguous

A clear statement of fact. A great deal of confusion can result from situations where statements are made that are unclear or vague.

Usage***** – A linguistic bequest of the long-running Ronseal adverts featuring a no-nonsense man fixated on his DIY task. Unsurprisingly, therefore, for the *No-nonsense manager* this is a moral and organisational yardstick.

See also **No-nonsense manager**

Tipping point
= n: a theory explaining how ideas are spread

Uncovered by the journalist Malcolm Gladwell in his bestselling book *The Tipping Point: How Little Things Can Make a Big Difference*, and formerly known as the 'snowball effect'.

Usage** – *Brand* and *Thesaurus managers* both of whom have heard of (but, perhaps, not yet read) Gladwell's book and see in it a handy all-purpose intellectual analogy to drop into conversations and presentations:'It's a *tipping point* kind of thing ... word-of-mouth epidemic ... little things making a big difference ... the new chaos theory ...'

See also **Brand manager**; **Effect, knock-on**; **Thesaurus manager**

Titanic, rearranging the deckchairs on the
= phrase: useless prevarication

Kate Winslet showed the way.

Usage **** – *No-nonsense managers* to curtail discussion in a *meeting*: 'We're getting nowhere fast here. You're just *rearranging the deckchairs on the Titanic*.' By contrast, for the *Machiavellian manager*, it was Winslet's fiancé – plutocrat, coward and determined survivor – who showed the way.

See also **Handbags, dancing round the**; **Machiavellian manager**; **No-nonsense manager**; **Shop, talking**

Tits out
= phrase: decisive; unalloyed

Semi-nakedness in the office always commands attention. A bold approach and one, it is worth underlining, that is not only available to the ladies.

Usage **** – *No-nonsense managers* recommending a strong tactical response to rectify a *problem*: 'No holds barred, mind you. We need to get our shoulders to the wheel and go *tits out* on this one.'

See also **No-nonsense manager**; **Problem**

Tits up
= phrase: awry; an unfavourable outcome

An embarrassing situation where one doesn't know where to look.

Usage ** – A down-to-earth phrase prized by straight-talking managers: 'We went to sleep at the wheel and it's all gone *tits up*, it has.'

See also **Pear-shaped, go**; **Sub-optimal**

Tongues, speaking in

= n: speech in no known language arising from a religious ecstasy

A sublime state employed for public displays of erudition.

Usage ** – Managers of their obscurantist *Marketing* colleagues who use piled-up jargon to demonstrate their professionalism: 'Couldn't understand a word. It was the usual mumbo-jumbo *speaking in tongues* twaddle.'

See also **Marketing manager**; **Show, dog and pony**

Touch base

= v: to communicate; exchange information

A one-sided conference.

Usage ***** – A vogue term in widespread use: 'I really need to *touch base* and chew the cud with you on this one.'

See also **Face time**; **Interface**; **Touchy-feely**

Touchy-feely

= adj: warm, empathetic

A show of tenderness that can send a shiver down the spine.

Usage *** – The self-designated management style of the *Californian manager* and a term of disparagement for everyone else: 'There was nothing of substance at all. It was all just fluffy *touchy-feely* nonsense.'

See also **Californian manager**; **Huddle**

Tour d'horizon

= n: overview

A panorama that requires a French-speaking guide.

Usage * – *Thesaurus managers* presenting an outline or report.

See also **Overview**; **Thesaurus manager**

Track record

= n: a person's past performance

A *curriculum vitae* always tells a story – and there are many ways to tell a story.

Usage *** – In job adverts for a wide variety of positions: 'Your *CV* will show an enviable/proven/successful *track record* of achievement and will spell out the story of your success.'

See also **CV**

Training manager

Earnest and perpetually *enthusiastic*, he is sustained by a thoroughgoing belief in professional and *personal growth*. His search is for meaning in the office. He is always honest and sincere; his watchwords are '*learnings*', '*making a dif-ference*' and '*ownership*'. For him his colleagues are actors on the stage of life where 'Every Day is the *Opportunity* to Give the Performance of a Lifetime'[§] and 'A goal is a dream with a deadline'. He is their coach and *mentor* guiding them towards fulfilment in a 'positive *proactive* learning environment' (including acting out scenes from *Macbeth*, role play, creating collages, yomping across countryside in the cold, and so on and so on). He is, of course, mocked by everyone and should, if at all possible, be avoided.[§§]

See also **Alarm bells ringing, set; Assertive; Boat, in the same; Buy in; Change; Contribution; Difference, making a; Enthusiasm; Feedback; Growth, personal; Influencer; Inspirational; Learnings; Mentor; Opportunity; Own; Proactive; Problem; Skill set; Work, dirty; Workshop**

[§] Never-to-be-forgotten *inspirational* advice taken from a finalist (aka Bonnie Tyler) on *Stars in their Eyes*.

[§§] The collective noun for *Training managers* is a compliment.

Trenches, in the
= phrase: active

A posting that is dreaded by the sane and healthy.

Usage *** – *Sales managers* and *Samurai managers*.

See also **Sales manager**; **Samurai manager**

Trojan, working like a
= phrase: exceptionally industrious

A state of self-pity brought about by a period of sustained heroic achievement that has gone unrecognised and unrewarded.

Usage * – Managers, with a what-can-I-do grimace, to justify their continued employment: 'I'd love to help but I'm already *working like a Trojan* at the moment' (translation: 'Why don't you go and boil your head?'). It is useful in the office to have a supply of 'working like a . . .' analogies.

See also **Dog, working like a**; **Navvy, working like a**; **Slave driver**; **Stakhanovite, working like a**

Troops, the
= n: soldiers or armed unit

A force that, ideally, is loyal, trained and *motivated*.

Usage ***** – An approved Offlish formula for a '*team*' used mostly by condescending senior managers to joshingly describe their underlings: 'I'll rally *the troops* for a *powwow*.' The *Sales manager* has control of the 'front line' or 'crack' *troops*; *Samurai managers*, on the other hand, tend not to see this as a figure of speech.

See also **Guys**; **Huddle**; **Motivation**; **Powwow**; **Sales manager**; **Samurai manager**; **Team**

Trouser
= v: to filch

A stunt requiring a great deal of practice to achieve a professional standard.

Usage* – Unhappy managers describing the board's allocation to itself of a jaw-dropping, supersized annual bonus.

See also **Cat, fat**; **Pockets, deep**

Truth
= n: the established facts

As fiercely debated in the office as in academia.

Usage** – *PR managers* as a statement: 'The *truth* is . . .' (translation: 'Today's story is . . .'); nervous managers questioning the veracity of a rumour.

See also **Honest, to be**; **Public Relations manager**

Tweak
= v: to amend; make fine adjustments

A process of adjustment that can result cumulatively in a substantial alteration.

Usage*** – Hard-pressed *CEOs* briefing journalists ahead of a major policy announcement: 'This is not a *strategy U-turn*. We are merely addressing legitimate concerns by examining the wider context and giving a little *tweak* to our tactics in the light of new market conditions' (translation: 'It's a *U-turn*'); overworked managers: 'It just needs a little *tweaking*, a little fine tuning and it'll be there' (translation: 'I'll get started on it tomorrow').

See also **CEO**; **Strategy**; **U-turn**

24/7
= adv: 24 hours/seven days a week

A division of time: there are seven days in every week and 24 hours in every day. For some this is a comfort; for others a hindrance.

Usage ***** – This is a dark term that should trigger a Pavlovian response: an immediate and unrenounceable distrust of the user. Anyone prepared to use the phrase without an ironic inflection is almost certain to be a thousand-yard-stare *workaholic* sociopath whose entire existence begins and ends with the office. Such individuals are dangerous and should, if at all possible, be avoided. They can only bring trouble; or worse, generate even more work for you. It is used habitually by *Hungry managers* who never relax and will earnestly inform candidates: 'We are a *full-on 24/7* company. We like to go gangbusters. Are you hungry? Can you rise to the *challenge* and *hit the ground running?*'

See also **Always-on**; **Challenge**; **CrackBerry**; **Full-on**; **Hit the ground running**; **Hungry manager**; **Workaholic**

USP
= acronym: Unique Selling Proposition/Point

An elastic concept.

Usage **** – Executives, *Brand*, *Sales* and *Marketing managers* habitually – all with vigour and all without recourse to a dictionary: executives using an accepted formula to brief the press and the City; *Brand* and *Marketing managers* in Powerpoint presentations where the phrase is buried in the usual farrago of jargon, shaky reasoning and false promises; *Sales managers* in pitches where 'unique' has the meaning 'pretty good'.

See also **Brand manager**; **Marketing manager**; **Sales manager**

Unironic manager

A dedicated worker who is perpetually cheerful and genial.
For him the glass is always at least 'half full'. He has achieved
a blessed, almost nirvanic, state where the accepted language
and mores of the office have fused with his personality.[§]
This dictionary is, more or less, his entire vocabulary, and
normal conversation with him is impossible. Thus for him
the tough really *do* get going '*when the going gets tough*',
and the '*customer* is *always right*'. Indeed, it may be true
that his entire life is conducted in Offlish (but as he would
inevitably add, '*Let's not go there*'). Unless the purpose
is Offlish research he should, therefore, if at all possible,
be avoided.

See especially **Absolutely!; Appropriate; At the end of the
day; Customer is always right, the; Doomsday scenario;
80/20 rule; Flagpole, run it up the; Fruit, low-hanging;
Gas, cooking with; Hymn sheet, singing from the same;
Let's not go there; Off-line; Park it (but keep the motor
running); Partnership; Picture, big; Potato, hot;
Proactive; Prophecy; Rocket science; Space, watch this;
Stops, the; Struggle; Throw the baby out with the bath
water, don't; Tick in the box; Wash its face; When the
going gets tough, the tough get going**

[§] The collective noun for *Unironic managers* is a bromide.

Unthinkable, thinking the
= phrase: considering every possibility

An impossible task and a regular request.

Usage **** – The kind of job adverts headed 'Achievers' or
'Calling the Best of the Best' that demand '*thinking outside
the square*' or a '*blue-sky*' approach; managers who describe

themselves as 'creative'; also cynical *management consultants* who didn't bother to read the brief – or who *did* read the brief and found it too difficult: 'We've come at it from a different angle, although it's still context-sensitive. It's a bit left field but we've been *thinking the unthinkable* ...'

See also **Box, thinking outside the**; **Management consultant**; **Off-the-wall**; **Square, thinking outside the**; **Thinking, blue-sky**

Up for it?
= phrase: display unrestrained enthusiasm

A question to which one generally knows the answer.

Usage**** – *Sales managers* giving a pep talk; also managers imitating, for a moment, the rabid *enthusiasm* of the *Hungry manager* in order to make the correct impression.

See also **Enthusiasm**; **Hungry manager**; **Sales manager**

Upscale
= v: to increase resources

A decision that is often pregnant with political tensions.

Usage**** – Directors and senior managers in response to criticism of a particular piece of work: 'We're going to have to *upscale* our efforts on this one' (translation: 'I have hopelessly underestimated the amount of time/people/money required for this and now I am throwing time/people/money at it like billy-o in order to prevent this turning into a complete disaster').

See also **Downscale**

Upside
= n: an improvement

An optimistic assessment that is always a cause for celebration.

Usage**** – *Sales managers*, choosing optimism over realism:

'It's not all doom and gloom. Not by any manner of means. There's no magic wand but there's definitely some *upside* here.'§

See also **Downside**; **News, good**; **Numbers, the**

§ In publishing, '*upside*' refers to the predicted sales of a book acquired from an author for little money. Elsewhere, the word 'fleeced' is used.

Upwards, managing
= phrase: influencing one's superiors

Arguably, the most important office skill to master.

Usage *** – Management handbooks invariably underline that the relationship between manager and managed should be open and positive and, ideally, should involve a regular and candid exchange of views, but the reality is more likely to consist of a daily round of humiliations – providing coffee, laughing at familiar jokes, nodding at hobbyhorse opinions, consistently covering up his mistakes, and so on and so on. It is a term used by managers everywhere.

See also **Scapegoat**

User, end
= n: the person using the product or service

An individual without influence: the customer, the consumer, you or me.

Usage *** – '*Consumer-driven*' executives who tend to think of people as potential contributors to '*the bottom line*'; *Marketing* and *IT managers* who prefer to think of *people* as an item on a chart or symbol in a computer programme.

See also **Bottom line, the**; **Consumer-driven**; **IT manager**; **Marketing manager**; **People**

U-turn

= n: the turning of a vehicle; a reversal of policy

The safest time to undertake this tricky manoeuvre is when the road is completely clear and there is no one about.

Usage ** – Executives denying that the company's new initiative is an admission of failure; journalists crowing that the new initiative is an admission that the previous *strategy* was a colossal and costly mistake.

See also **Strategy**

Value-added

= adj: something additional to a product or service that makes it more valuable to the consumer

A miraculous transubstantiation.

Usage ***** – Cynical *Marketing managers* and *management consultants* suggesting yet another idea for duping the customer; pretentious job adverts for marketing positions; also desperate candidates hoping to say the right thing. It is also sometimes used as a noun (instead of the standard English 'benefit'): 'What is the *value-added* [or *value-add*'] in this?'

See also **Customer-facing**; **Management consultant**; **Marketing manager**

Values-driven

= adj: an ethical stance

A position that consists, more often than not, of nine parts audacity to one part morality.

Usage **** – Company literature and official PR statements (where *truth* is the first casualty); candidates who hope they are saying the right thing. (A variation is 'values-based'.)

See also **Truth**

Versatile

= adj: able to turn easily from one subject or task to another

A handy skill; however, a jack-of-all-trades is necessarily a master of none.

Usage*** – In job adverts where it is often twinned with 'a *can-do attitude*': 'You will be *versatile* and adaptable and will consistently demonstrate a *can-do attitude*' (translation: 'There is no job description. You will have to do whatever we tell you to do, no matter how crackpot or demeaning'). It also appears in *CVs* where it indicates that the candidate has no specialist knowledge, is desperate for employment, and is willing to do more or less anything.

See also **Attitude, can-do**; **CV**

Vision

= n: the act of seeing; imaginative insight; statesmanlike foresight

An evanescent will-o'-the-wisp that is difficult to capture with accuracy.

Usage***** – Self-promoting *CEOs*; senior managers echoing the *CEO*; cynical *management consultants*; *mission statements*; *Marketing managers* sprinkling *gravitas* on to a presentation; *Brand managers* with cult-like zealotry; also managers everywhere who mean 'idea' or 'proposal' or simply, 'what we are going to do'.

See also **Brand manager**; **CEO**; **Gravitas**; **Management consultant**; **Mission statement**; **Thinking, blue-sky**; **World, brave new**

Walk the walk

= phrase: put theory into practice

Harder than it at first appears: for instance, some actors practise a character's walk before they start to learn the lines.§

Usage***** – It is common in job adverts for sales positions:

'You will thrive on pressure. We are not interested in whether you can talk the talk. We want to know whether you can *walk the walk*. Can you? We aren't easily impressed. But, then again, neither are you.'

See also **Hit the ground running**

§ Sir Alec Guinness was one example.

War zone
= n: an area of conflict

Take care: the office can be a very dangerous place.

Usage *** – *Dramatic managers* describing a particularly bad-tempered *meeting*; *Samurai managers* describing office life.

See also **Bombshell**; **Dramatic manager**; **Meeting**; **Samurai manager**

Warning, health
= n: a caution against possible danger or difficulty

A bulletin published as a disclaimer against any future litigation.

Usage ** – Cautious managers everywhere: as an American colleague might say, 'covering their ass, big time'.

See also **Heads up**

Wash its face
= phrase: break even

A technical term.

Usage ***** – Worried *CEOs* questioning the board: 'This had better *wash its face*'; *Marketing managers* as a smokescreen assertion in the hope that no one will recognise that they are throwing away absurd amounts of money: 'This will definitely *wash its face*!'; also *Unironic managers* requesting a financial assessment.

See also **CEO**; **Marketing manager**; **Numbers, the**;
Unironic manager

Wavelength, on the same

= phrase: in agreement with a mode of thinking or communication

Cherish the moment.

Usage ** – Managers insisting, against all the evidence to the
contrary, that they are leading a united *team*. Also combative
managers making a point: 'We just don't seem to be *on the
same wavelength* on this one' (translation: 'You imbecile. You
oaf. You twit').

See also **Hymn sheet, singing from the same**; **Team**;
Thinking, joined-up

Well, scrubs up

= phrase: having an attractive appearance

A lecher's calling card.

Usage **** – Universally acknowledged as the appropriate
compliment for any out-of-hours office occasion that is
especially popular during the festive season with slavering male,
middle-aged managers.

See also **Bombshell**

What's what

= phrase: essential knowledge

The facts.

Usage * – *Sales managers*, to whoever will listen, describing
their overwhelming importance in the organisation.

See also **Coal face, at the**; **Eyes and ears**; **Sales manager**;
Sharp end, at the

Wheel, reinvent the
= phrase: an unnecessary repetition

The presence of the wheel in societies has been used by anthropologists as a sign of a sophisticated society and economy.

Usage ***** – Managers apportioning blame or reflecting on another corporate gaffe: 'Months of work and what's happened? They've *reinvented the wheel*!'

See also **Titanic, rearranging the deckchairs on the**

When the going gets tough, the tough get going
= phrase: a display of fortitude

Wisdom that has inspired T-shirt manufacturers everywhere.

Usage ***** – Amazingly there are still people who are able to use this lengthy phrase as if it is fresh-minted, both to themselves and their colleagues. The correct term for such a person is a moron. With either a smile or a grimace, the *Unironic manager* will happily proffer this insight.

See also **Unironic manager**

When you are in a hole stop digging
= phrase: don't make a situation worse than it already is

Good advice – unless you are burying something.

Usage ** – Managers everywhere in *meetings* poking fun at a hapless *colleague*.

See also **Colleague**; **Easy tiger!**; **Meeting**

Whip, crack the
= phrase: urge to action

A performance that is usually guaranteed to get attention.

Usage** – Unhappy managers to their *team*: 'I'm under-whelmed, *guys*. I'm not a happy bunny right now. You need to pull up your socks and *crack the whip* – or you'll be the ones reaping the whirlwind.' The influence of the circus in the office has long been underestimated.

See also **Guys**; **Team**

Whistles, bells and
= n: unnecessary refinements or features

A set of sound effects that is usually lacking in mellifluousness.

Usage*** – Calculating *Ambitious managers* pretending there is more to come; *Marketing managers* pretending that they haven't been wasting their time on trivialities (liaising with expensive design consultants, creating elaborate Powerpoint presentations, holding endless conversations about fonts and Pantone colours, and so on and so on); also *Sales managers* in disgust: 'This is nothing but fancy talk and *bells and whistles*, this is.'

See also **All-singing-all-dancing**; **Ambitious manager**; **Marketing manager**; **Sales manager**

Win/win
= adj: a favourable outcome for both sides in a negotiation

A principle that is not seen in nature.

Usage***** – Via the language of negotiation, the term 'We are looking for a *win/win*, gentlemen, not a *lose/lose*' has achieved widespread usage. For *Stephen R. Covey*, looking for '*win/win*' outcomes was one of the seven principal habits of the effective manager. It is often cited as the desiderata of managers and executives who would, in fact, gnaw through their own arm or sell their firstborn into slavery rather than lose out to a *colleague* or corporate opponent.

See also **Californian manager**; **Colleague**; **Stephen R. Covey**; **Lose/lose**

Wins, quick
= phrase: easy solutions to problems

A fillip in troubled times.

Usage **** – Hard-pressed managers everywhere: 'The word is that we need to deliver some *quick wins* for the *big boys* upstairs otherwise heads will roll. So let's start with the *low-hanging fruit.*'

See also **Big boys**; **Fruit, low-hanging**

Wood, dead
= n: useless persons or things

As every gardener knows, this must be cleared regularly to allow for new growth.

Usage *** – Executives and *HR managers* privately reflecting on the tedious but necessary work of clearance and reconstruction that lies ahead; uncaring journalists presenting a brutal public assessment.

See also **Axe**; **Downsize**; **Human Resources manager**; **People**; **Restructure**; **Talent, pool of**

Word on the street
= phrase: latest news or information

A cacophony that is almost always impossible to understand.

Usage *** – Managers over 30 ironically (nevertheless embarrassing themselves and everyone else); *Sales managers* without irony.

See also **Finger on the pulse**; **Sales manager**

Work, dirty
= n: an unpleasant task; employment

The daily round: a means of enrichment for the few; of paying the mortgage for the majority; for the deluded an *opportunity* for *personal growth*.

Usage *** – Unhappy managers describing their life, to which the cheery *Unironic manager* will inevitably add: '. . . but someone's got to do it!'

See also **Growth, personal**; **Opportunity**; **Unironic manager**

Workaholic
= n: a person addicted to work

A large mass of individuals with severe and apparently untreatable behavioural problems. It is of great public concern that their number is growing at such a rapid rate.

Usage ** – Managers enviously describing a more successful colleague: 'Of course, he's nothing but a *workaholic*. He's to be pitied really'; also managers lamenting their lot: 'You have to be a *workaholic* to survive here.'

See also **Always-on**; **CrackBerry**; **Hungry manager**

Work-life balance
= n: a harmonious lifestyle

A fairytale (created and popularised by magazine editors).

Usage **** – Exhausted managers glancing at the weekend supplements who daydream of *downshifting*; also naive candidates thereby talking themselves out of a job.

See also **Downshift**

Workshop

= n: a meeting for discussion

A convenient venue to confront, argue and obstruct.

Usage ** – Credulous *Californian* and *Training managers* for whom it is the answer to most *problems*; cynical *HR managers* and *management consultants* who know it is supposed to be the answer to *some problems*; everyone else in exasperation. It is also used as an ugly verb: 'Let's *workshop* this one and see what comes out the other end.'

See also **Californian manager**; **Human Resources manager**; **Management consultant**; **Problem**; **Training manager**

World, brave new

= n: the future

A fresh beginning, optimism being the fuel of life.

Usage * – *CEOs* presenting yet another new *strategy*; also *Thesaurus managers* who cannot stop themselves from explaining the Shakespearean origin of the phrase and giving a brief synopsis of Huxley's dystopian novel (as the room rapidly empties).

See also **CEO**; **Strategy**; **Thesaurus manager**; **Vision**

World-class

= adj: among the best in the world

An extraordinary standard: good; possibly *very* good

Usage *** – Burdened *CEOs* gambling on the success of a new initiative: 'This will be a market-leading, *world-class* product/ service'; *IT managers* routinely of any new software or hardware development; *Marketing managers* on just about anything, as their natural mode is the language of *hype*: 'This is literally *world-class*.' Remember: exaggeration never does harm to corporate aspirants so long as it is delivered noisily and with striking self-confidence.

See also **Ante**; **Breed, best in**; **CEO**; **Hype**; **IT manager**; **Marketing manager**

Worldly-wise manager

An experienced 'old hand' who is, by his own admission, a 'bit long in the tooth' and has 'been around the block . . . seen it all . . . been there, done that, *and* bought the T-shirt'. He has put in the 'hard graft' and has been 'producing the goods' for many years. A windbag and gossiper, he has, however, fashioned a comfortable company berth for himself from which to dispense unsolicited platitudinous advice. By his own admission he 'doesn't miss a trick', and on any topic he will offer a 'word to the wise'. He is scorned by all and should, if at all possible, be avoided.[§]

See also **Boat, rock the**; **Change**; **Days, halcyon**; **Keep an even keel**; **Keep one's powder dry**; **Left hand not knowing what the right hand is doing**; **No such thing as a free lunch**; **Put one's head above the parapet**; **Rome wasn't built in a day**; **Rule of thumb**; **Talk**; **Teach your grandmother to suck eggs, don't**; **Sword, double-edged**

[§] The collective noun for *Worldly-wise managers* is a saw.

Wow factor
= noun: something worthy of admiration

An immediate positive response to something which is so overwhelming that words are insufficient to describe the effect.

Usage **** – Correctly identified by *Tom Peters* as critical to achieving business success. It is the Offlish equivalent of Archimedes's 'Eureka!' and is used by the *Californian manager* as an '*inspirational*' standard: 'The question I always ask myself is: "Does it have the *wow factor*?"'

See also **Californian manager**; **Inspirational**; **Tom Peters**

Yes
= adv & n: affirmation or confirmation

Almost always the right answer.

Usage * – Managers everywhere – like nodding dogs on the back shelf of an old Cortina – replying to their boss, or in *meetings* with senior managers or executives.

See also **Meeting**; **No**; **Yes-man**

Yes-man
= n: an acquiescent person

An individual who believes that obedience is a prime virtue.

Usage *** – Managers describing (more successful) *colleagues*; *mavericks* describing anyone.

See also **Colleague**; **Maverick**; **Puppet**; **Yes**

Z
= n: the 26th letter of the alphabet

The final letter of the alphabet. The end.

Usage *** – Humourless executives who think it is amusing to use Americanisms – 'OK. That's it. We have our *ducks in a row*. I think we've covered everything from *A to Zee*' – and to underline the end of a discussion with a hand-signalled 'FULL STOP'.

See also **A-Z**; **Ducks in a row**; **Humour, sense of**

Appendix One

Humour, a sense of: Examples

The Marketing manager

Q Why does a Marketing manager need two windows?

A So that he has a different view in the afternoon.

The Sales manager

Q How do you know when a Sales manager is lying?

A Because his lips are moving.

Appendix Two

The Jargon of the Management Consultant

The following list is a small sample of the kind of jargon that is created by management consultants. These are, for the most part, intelligent people with too much time on their hands, and the majority of these words and phrases are manufactured with a pronounced element of ironic, look-at-me knowingness, which makes clear that they aren't intended to be taken altogether seriously. Unfortunately, many of their clients do not understand irony and, therefore, these linguistic confections – many of which originate in the US – can achieve a wider currency through earnest repetition.

Adhocracy – an organisation that is managed by a series of temporary teams for specific tasks

Alpha geek – the person who is the most technically proficient in the office

Analysis paralysis – spending too much time researching rather than getting on with something

Asteroid event – an event that almost brings about the extinction of a company

Bad cosmetics – any action or event whereby a company would get bad publicity

BEER – Bitchin' Extra Effort Reward

Betamaxed – where one technology has taken over from another

BFO – Blinding Flash of the Obvious

BHAGs – Big Hairy Audacious Goals

Black-collar workers – creative types who tend to wear black clothes

Blame shift – to assign responsibility

Blow one's buffer – to lose one's train of thought

Bobbleheading – communal agreement in a meeting

Boiling the ocean - to expend a lot of effort
Brain dump - a briefing
Bricks and mortar - a traditional business
CLM - Career-Limiting Move
Chips and salsa - hardware and software
Clicks and mortar - a traditional business that has successfully
   integrated internet services
Cobweb site - an unused, out-of-date website
Cube farm - an office filled with cubicles
Data dump - a briefing
Decommission - to sack someone
Decruit - to sack someone
Dehire - to sack someone
De-install - to sack someone
E-dress - email address
E-load - the volume of email that a person receives
E-tailing - electronic retailing
Egosurf - to google one's own name
Elvis year - the peak of someone's/something's popularity
Event horizon - the point of no return
Facilitation competence - competence
Going postal - to lose one's temper
Halo effect - the beneficial effect of a bestselling product or
   service on another product or service
Intel - useful information (from the novel *Snow Crash* and
   popularised by Keifer Sutherland's Jack Bauer in *24*)
Managerial courage - taking decisions
Megadigm - a big change
Metrics - information
Negative growth - a loss
Negative profit - a loss
Next-generation - the best of its kind
Ohnosecond - the fraction of a second in which someone
   realises that they have made an irretrievable mistake
Open-collar worker - people who work from home
Open the kimono - to disclose information
Pushback - a response

Re-purposing – reusing published material for a website
Root cause analysis – analysis
SWAG – Simply Wild Ass Guess
TON – Total Outsourcing Nirvana
Uninstall – to sack someone
Uplevel – to raise standards
Upskilling – to acquire new skills
User-centric – created for the use of the customer
VCs – Venture Capitalists
Visioning – having ideas
WOMBAT – Waste Of Money, Bandwidth And Time
Zerotasking – having nothing to do (via a *New Yorker* cartoon)
(In the) Zone – to concentrate and work productively

Appendix Three

The Sickie: Planning and Implementation

1 Success depends on a degree of chutzpah and a thorough knowledge of the boss's diary.

2 On the designated day it is best to ring very early so as to have the best possible chance of reaching the answerphone rather than anybody who might ask awkward questions (such as, 'I'm surprised you are up at all after the vast quantity of booze you drank at last night's party' or 'Your holiday starts tomorrow, doesn't it?').

3 With the aid of a thickened first-thing-in-the-morning wheeze, explain as concisely as possible that something 'resembling' 'flu has struck during the night and will necessitate immediate bed rest otherwise the danger is that the entire office will be infected. Do not elaborate and get off the phone as quickly as possible. A sympathetic response can be a dangerous invitation to embellishment.

4 Once this unpleasant but necessary task is completed, it should be followed by a vigorous pounding of the air with a bunched fist and a capering jig of delight.

5 Attention can then be turned to coffee or tea, a substantial breakfast and the day's TV listings.

6 Finally, use a few minutes of the day to mark your diary for the next occasion when you anticipate that you will require rest and recuperation.

Acknowledgements

I owe a huge debt of thanks to Aurea Carpenter and Rebecca Nicolson and everyone at Short Books for their enthusiasm, expertise and tolerance.

My thanks also to all at Faber for their unstinting efforts but especially Kate Beal, Diana Broccardo, Joann Jacobs, Neal Price and Dave Woodhouse.

This book, however, wouldn't have been completed without the constant encouragement and practical assistance of my wife. Mary, in this as in so many other ways, I cannot thank you enough. My mother, Irene, I thank for her patience. *Ducks in a Row* is dedicated to both of you.

In addition, for their valued contribution, I'd like to thank the following: Simon Benham, John Bond, Chris Cannam (for IT know-how), Helen Cannam, Iain Chapple, Barry Clark, Karen Davies, Ben Dunn (who, happily, didn't go to Surrey), Graham Edmonds (who was present at the beginning), Jane Harris (who lobbied persistently), Mike Jacobs, Gordon Kerr, Douglas McCabe, Kes Nielsen, Jazz Mack-Smith, Martin Palmer, Chris Rushby, Kate Summerscale, Martin Toseland, Toby Watson, Jon Woolcott and Simon Youngs.

All the errors are, of course, mine and I have left a handful in the book so that those who are of a certain bent may enjoy the thrill of the hunt. Short Books would be delighted to receive your correspondence on this matter although, unlike the excellent – although sadly now defunct – tradition of Bible publishers, there are, to my knowledge, no cash prizes on offer.

Bibliography

Scott Adams, *The Dilbert Principle* (Boxtree, 1996)
Hans Christian Andersen, *Fairy Tales* (Penguin Books, 2004)
Stephen Bayley, *A Dictionary of Idiocy* (Gibson Square, 2003)
Ambrose Bierce, *The Devil's Dictionary* (Bloomsbury, 2003)
Brewer's Dictionary of Phrase and Fable (Wordsworth, 2001)
Madeleine Bunting, *Willing Slaves* (Fourth Estate, 2004)
www.buzzwhack.com
James Cochrane, *Between You and I* (Icon Books, 2003)
Collins English Dictionary (HarperCollins, 2005)
Collins Concise Thesaurus (HarperCollins, 2003)
William Donaldson, *I'm Leaving You Simon, You Disgust Me . . .*
    (Weidenfeld & Nicolson, 2003)
Encarta World English Dictionary (Bloomsbury, 1999)
Harry G Frankfurt, *On Bullshit* (Princeton University Press,
    2005)
www.google.com
John Humphrys, *Lost for Words* (Hodder & Stoughton, 2004)
Albert Jack, *Red Herrings and White Elephants* (Metro, 2004)
George Orwell, *Politics and the English Language*, in *Why I
    Write* (Penguin Books, 2004)
Nigel Rees, *A Word in Your Shell-Like* (HarperCollins, 2004)
Ian Sansom, *Ring Road* (Harper Perennial, 2005)
    – a work of genius: seek it out today
Don Watson, *Gobbledygook* (Atlantic Books, 2004)
Francis Wheen, *How Mumbo-Jumbo Conquered the World*
    (HarperCollins, 2004)
www.worldwidewords.com

I should also like to make clear that none of the authors in this list are personal friends. Our relationship is more straightforward: I stole from them. I hope that they will forgive my impertinence.

Index

For reasons of space, a number of important words have been omitted that are a conspicuous feature of life in the office – such as Anger, Enemies, Hate, Insanity, Intolerance, Lies, Politics, Sex, Violence.

notes